Humor Helps!

What People Say:

"Hooray for Brother Craig! He's a First, a Last, a One of a Kind!"

Marty Ingels

☺

"There's no crying in the chapel with Brother around. Read this laugh-out-loud religiously."

Linda Barnard, humor columnist, *The Toronto Sun*

☺

"We discovered some things about ourselves and our society by reading this book."

Don and Alleen Nilsen; director, International Society for Humor Studies; editor, *International Journal of Humor Research.*

☺

"This guy is the Dave Barry of Monkdom."

Pam Stone, standup comic

☺

"There are lots of funny books, and lots of books about humor, but there are few funny books about humor. This is one of the best. It explains why humor is good for you, while it keeps you laughing. "

John Morreall, Ph.D. author and president of Humorworks Seminars

"Brother Craig has a wonderful sense of humor. How lucky for us he wishes to share it with the world."

Mary McBride, humor author and gag writer for Phyllis Diller and Joan Rivers

"This book is a marvelous mixture of mirth, merriment and meaning. Read it and reap!"

Allen Klein, humor author and speaker

"I laughed out loud. And for a Norwegian, that's saying something! Brother Craig's style and wit will hook you. He'll show you the twist around every corner and help to add smiles to your life."

John Kinde, humor specialist

"Brother Craig is the funniest person in the whole wide world. He really is!"

Aunt Twaddle, Brother Craig's maiden aunt and loveable nag

"A jester may be first in the Kingdom of Heaven,
because he has diminished the sadness of human life."

Rabbi Max Nussbaum

Humor Helps!

*The benefits of humor,
laughter, and being funny.*

Brother Craig
The Mirthful Monk

Photographs by Brother John Raymond

Woodbridge Press / Santa Barbara

Published and Distributed by

Woodbridge Press Publishing Company
815 De La Vina Street
Post Office Box 102
Santa Barbara, California 93102

Distributed simultaneously in the United States and Canada.
Printed in the United States of America.

Library of Congress Cataloging-in-Publication Data:

Craig, Brother.
 Humor Helps! : the benefits of humor, laughter, and being funny / Brother Craig : photographs by Brother John Raymond.

  p. cm.

 ISBN 0-88007-219-9 (alk. paper)

 1. Wit and humor—Religious aspects—Christianity. 2. Craig, Brother. I. Title.

BR115.H84C73 1998
230'.002'07—dc21   98-14694
                                                    CIP

Inside photographs by Brother John Raymond.
Cover photographs by Robert Mayer.

Why am I laughing at the dedications?

I Sincerely Dedicate this Book ...

To all cab drivers, everywhere.

To Donald Trump, hoping you'll send a donation. You see, we want to build a library here at the monastery—and after all, I did read all three of your books.

To Steven Spielberg. Call me.

To the nice people at Gulden's Mustard. Can't I be on a commercial?

To my Aunt Twaddle who paid me to add her name here.

Acknowledgments

There are many people I need to thank. Fortunately for you, I can't remember most of them. I do remember that I thank Gene Perret for writing the Foreword which is very interesting. Be sure to read about him on Page 159. I also thank all the fine people who risked their reputation writing "blurbs" about this book. I especially thank Brother John Raymond for taking the photos that are found inside here somewhere. I also thank him for his help, encouragement and for many funny additions to this book. I thank my writing teacher, Elizabeth Ann Paulin, whose fine teaching has enriched my writing, though none of it comes through in this book. I thank also the many groups around the country which have invited me to give talks on the benefits of humor. Finally, I thank Dr. Howard Weeks, publisher at Woodbridge Press, who, in a moment of distraction, agreed to publish this book. He'll regret it.

Table of Contents

"If he laughs well, he is a good man." Fyodor Dostoyevski

This is me, one of the Monks Brothers,
introducing you to Gene Perret.

Foreword

I surely endorse the premise of this book—humor helps. Brother Craig has done much research to find quotes from people, living and dead, who tell us that humor is good for us, body and soul, mind and spirit, inwardly and outwardly.

It should be obvious. Suppose you go into a party and notice two groups of people. One of these groups is laughing, slapping their thighs, holding their sides, having a great time. The other bunch is kicking the dog, throwing food at one another, and scratching one another's eyes and pulling each other's hair. Which bunch are you going to migrate towards?

We all want to have fun, be joyous and feel good. And nothing feels as good as laughter. To paraphrase a famous commercial of a few years ago: "You only go around once in life. Grab for all the giggles you can get."

I've been around humor most of my life. I've known and worked for some of the legends of the comedy profession. I've written for them and traveled with them. I've seen first hand what the gift of comedy can do.

I've seen a laugh brighten up a person in a hospital bed.

I've watched a couple of wisecracks lift the spirits of some pretty gloomy wounded veterans in makeshift military hospitals. I sat in the audience and watched as some glorious comedy raised the morale of fighting men and women stuck in some war theatre, homesick for their loved ones. Laughter has that kind of therapeutic value.

But those are extreme circumstances. Humor serves each of us daily. It's not an anomaly. Not something we call on only when there's no other escape. No. It's there for all of us all of the time.

I remember when I was feeling self pity (and taking it out on anyone who didn't share my feelings) at a time when I had received some bad news about my health. The immediate treatment was a medicinal patch I had to wear on my body. I whined and complained and made everyone around me miserable because this patch kept coming loose because of all the hair on my body.

I said, "No matter where I put this dumb thing, the hair makes it come loose."

My daughter offered a solution. She said, "Why don't you put it on top of your head?"

I laughed. Not only because I had to admit my hair was thinning (actually had thinned long ago), but also because I realized that forgetting about my sense of humor was not helping my health. It was making my problems worse.

From then on I laughed and felt better.

Laughter isn't the magic bullet that will cure all of your problems or solve the world's ills. Some of those things we'll always have with us. But a hearty sense of humor is much better than the alternative.

Laugh and be happy. During his troubles, President Lincoln said, "I laugh so that I don't cry."

That's one of the real benefits of humor—the more time you spend feeling good, joyous and with a laugh in your heart, the less time you'll have to feel the opposite of those.

So have some laughs in this book. Humor Helps!

Gene Perret

Allow me to introduce you to this angel—

Introduction

This is an *Apologia pro Libro Sua*—which is Latin for an "Apology for his book." Of course, apology can mean defense, and let's just hope that's all it means here.

There were times (brief moments of depression at 4:00 a.m.) when I thought I should chuck this book. It did occur to me that people would think it weird that a monk wrote a book on humor. But I had an experience that caused me to throw out all doubts. The experience was very simple—I was away from the monastery for a while. I went on a week-long speaking tour and learned a few things. Here they are:

—People are very tense.

—People need to lighten up.

—The only funny people I met while traveling was a guy who sold powdered motor oil through the mail and a wait-ress (I mean table attendee) in St. Louis who could balance four glasses of water on one wrist.

So I came home and dug out this manuscript, stuffed it into an envelope and mailed it to a publisher. I also decided to try to convince the people who invite me for speaking engagements to let me speak on "Laughter as a Way of Life," or another helpful topic: "How To Get a Tax Break for Collecting Live Beavers." As we all know, deep down in our hearts, collecting live beavers is what we want to do.

I guess I should tell you that this book perfectly reflects me, the author. It's mixed up. As far as I can tell (though I never reread what I write, because it would be too humiliating), it's about 25 percent self-help and 85 percent humorous stuff that is not related to other stuff, or to anything. But allow me to say (just try and stop me) that the funny stuff parts may not seem very self-help-ish (they're not), but if they make you laugh (which is unlikely) then I'm practicing what I believe about humor—that it's really good for you, so good (and because I care, really) that I've written this funny stuff for you. As I said, the book's mixed up.

But this is a great book. An extraordinary book. Soon to be a "Best Seller." Never has a greater book been written. (How am I doing so far?)

This book will change your life. (It'll probably make it worse.) It's a very funny book. See Jane. See Spot run. See Jane scream at Spot. (The writing program on my computer says this introduction is up to second grade reading level.)

This book was written over a long period of time. Almost a whole week. A lot of thought went into it—but very little comes out. I wrote it to help humanity. I found it real easy to write (except this introduction which took three weeks).

Being funny has always been a part of my life. I could laugh before I could walk. (Every baby can.) Humor runs in my family. Just the other night it ran through the living room.

I hope everyone who buys this book will enjoy it and buy several hundred more. Seriously, though I hate that word, thank you for buying this book.

And, finally, allow me to conclude this my telling you about Anna Russell's grandmother. (Anna Russell has spent her life doing comic singing especially comic opera type singing.) She lived in France (her grandmother, that is) and spoke French very badly. Many years ago she was riding in a carriage and thought that the spring of the carriage was broken. She shouted to the driver, "Cochon! Cochon! Descendez de votre boîte. Le printemps de votre mouche est cassé." Which translated means, I think, "Pig! Pig! Come down from your box. The springtime of your insect is broken."

Well, here we are, still in the Introduction, where I should be introducing you, the reader, to the book. Or should I be introducing the book to you? Or should I tell you about Kaiser Kurt II who was eight feet tall, had a different color mustache for each day of the week, wore a helmet with a carrot shaped spike and invented peanut butter fondue? Now he was quite a guy. So loved by his people that each year on his birthday they would gather around the palace and play solitaire until Dawn arrived. Then they would play solitaire with Dawn.

Then people would dance for seven or eight minutes and talk about the country's favorite movie, "Tapioca for Two." Then, at last, Kaiser Kurt would come to the palace balcony. It took him a long time to scale the wall of the palace. The balcony didn't have a door. Shortly after the Kaiser reached the balcony he would pull up his wife, the Kaiserette, Brunwiga the Tubby. He'd pull her up using a rope tied around her hat. When she reached the balcony it would sag due to her weight. The people cheered. Then everyone went to an all-you-can-eat kiwi drivethru restaurant. The Kaiser paid. He was that kind of Kaiser.

You may think that this Introduction has wandered off the subject. But really it has. The point is, what our world needs today is a C.F.C.P. That is, a Center for Certified Peasants. This has, as all scholars know, been long overdue. This center would serve the international journalistic community immensely. I'll explain. The center would have on hand several genuine and certified Eastern European peasants. (From no specific country, just generic peasants.) There would be men with beards, broad shoulders and beards on their broad shoulders.

All the men would be named Boris. The women would be

fat, square and wear babushka kerchiefs. They would all be named Lola Lovette. All the peasants would talk nonstop, wave their hands and demand their rights. On Tuesdays they would demand their lefts. Like all true peasants they would grow only hay and would bundle it into decorative bundles shaped like six-sided wine glasses, as is customary among peasants.

The value of this center is obvious. When journalists, reporters and hairdressers want to know what generic peasants think about politics, hay seeds or toenail polish for salamanders—they just go over to the center and amid the yelling, beet-soup throwing and hay bundling they get valuable information. I felt that the need for the Center for Certified Peasants was so urgent, so great and so unnecessary that I had to give the space here in this Introduction to speak out about it.

Brother Craig

"*True humor springs more from the heart*
   than from the head; it is not contempt, its essence is love."
                                          Thomas Carlyle

This is the best picture of me.

Humor's What We Need

I must tell you right off that this chapter is really good because it has a lot of quotations.

Life is serious, has problems, etc. Humor helps us to take this serious life not too seriously. Humor helps us to live in a lighthearted way. As Bill Cosby says, "You can turn painful situations around through laughter. If you can find humor in anything—even poverty—you can survive it."

Another talented comedian, Red Skelton, said, "Live by this credo: have a little laugh at life and look around you for happiness instead of sadness. Laughter has always brought me out of unhappy situations. Even in your darkest moment, you usually can find something to laugh about if you try hard enough." And, of course, Will Rogers said, "We are all here for a spell. Get all the good laughs you can." Then, again, my dear Aunt Mackel said, "Never use whip cream for tooth paste." Where was I? And, furthermore (don't you dare stop reading), Brian Derry says, "Humor provides us with a valuable tool for maintaining inner strength in the midst of utter turmoil." And here's a quote from David Brenner—"There's a correlation between bad times and the rise of comedy. People need the escape." Ain't it the truth? And Rollo May says, "Humor is the healthy way of feeling a 'distance' between one's self and the problem, a way of standing off and looking at one's problems with perspective."

I'm convinced that there can be no humor for the real atheist—for him or her this life is all there is—that's tragic, serious and totally unhumorous! So it is the believer who has the right to be funny! As Henny Youngman said, "I tried to be an atheist, but I gave up—they have no holidays."

Perhaps humor's greatest help to life is it's ability to "throw off" anger. Mary McNorton tells us, "Humor is the oil that keeps the engine of society from getting overheated." And Goldie Hawn says, "Comedy breaks down walls. It opens up people." Next time someone starts to get upset, frustrated, annoyed or angry with you—try humor.

Studies have shown that it's impossible for two people to argue while lying on their backs, on the floor. It's sort of the same with humor. If we laugh instead of yelling, there will be less fighting in the world. If we turn to humor instead of weapons, there will be fewer wars. No, it's not as simple as that, but humor does help. Let's not forget the wise words of Alan Alda—"When people are laughing, they're generally not killing one another."

Humor and having a good sense of humor helps us to have a correct perspective on life, on ourselves. Humor helps us not to take ourselves too seriously. Perhaps that's humor's greatest help. We are far too serious about ourselves. We need to lighten up, folks!

G. K. Chesterton said, "Angels can fly because they take themselves lightly. Satan fell by force of gravity." We need to take ourselves lightly. Of course, pride doesn't like this. Pride wants us to be ponderous, to strive to comprehend fully our own greatness lest we not have the proper awe and respect for ourselves. But pride isn't any fun. Pride is a dull lie that tries to convince us that we are the center of the universe, when everyone knows that Boston is!

Or, as William Arthur said, "To make mistakes is human; to stumble is commonplace; to be able to laugh at yourself is maturity."

Or, as my Aunt Mackel (again) said, "Shut up and eat your okra."

Humor relates to humility. No, the words aren't related. Humor refers to the old medical theory of the four humors of a person's constitution. Humility relates to humus as in earth, being passive, accepting rain, sunshine, etc. But the concepts of humor and humility do relate. Not taking one's self too seriously is the mark of a humble man. (Not taking the same guy too seriously is the mark of a wise woman.)

A humble person will see humor in his or her (sounds like matching towels) own self—in what he or she does, thinks, etc. Humor and humility are interwoven and also I can't think of anything else to write about them, except that having a sense of humor will help you laugh when you feel humiliated. End of sermon, at least for now.

Going back to the early years of Christianity (in the totally disorganized way I have with historical research, scholarship and lawn croquet), we find St. Jerome who wrote, "I amuse myself by laughing at the grubs, owls and crocodiles." Then, again, I myself have seldom rolled on the floor laughing uncontrollably over the antics of grubs, but to each his own.

Why were the saints cheerful, humorous and funny? (Why are so many holy, God-loving people today so humorous?) Because they trusted God to get them safely through this life and they cooperated so they could get into Heaven in the next life. They didn't take life too seriously. They discovered that they could take or endure this life better if they added humor. They were happy and cheerful by choice. We should be happy and cheerful and so happy and cheerful that we are downright funny!

Or, as John F. Kennedy said, "There are three things which are real: God, human folly and laughter. The first two are beyond our comprehension, so we must do what we can with the last one." And, while I'm quoting, I mustn't forget Harvey Cox, who believes, "Holy laughter is a gift of grace. It is the human spirit's last defense against banality and despair. Sometimes I think that, along with martyred missionaries, comedians—those of the gentle type—can be God's emissaries in a mean-spirited time like ours." And, finally, allow me to end this chapter with the words of the great G. K. Chesterton— "The Bible tells us to love our neighbors, and also to love our enemies; probably because they are generally the same people."

"Prepare for mirth, for mirth becomes a feast."
Bill Shakespeare

Okay, so I'll never get on "Touched by an Angel."

And God said, "So laugh a little"

Actually it was Molly Picon, the Jewish actress, who said it. She wrote a book and gave it that title. Doesn't matter. God says it, too. "Laugh a little." Trust me, I should know. I'm a monk. God wants you to laugh and be happy. He wants you to have a life of joy and cheerfulness. Yeah, life is not easy. God knows that, but if you laugh it will help you get through life. It might even help you get through the day!

It's like this. If you laugh and don't take situations too seriously (the way you have been, I know), then you'll be kinder, you'll stop getting impatient and won't say (or think) nasty things. If you laugh and take yourself less seriously, then you'll be nice and humble. And everyone likes humble people. No one likes proud and arrogant people. Sure, we love them, but we don't like them. Please laugh and take other people less seriously—yes, I mean that; when they're angry, humor them; when they're unkind, smile at them; and when they are very, very difficult—feed them! But don't take the unkind, nasty, rotten things people do too seriously. (By the way, when people are yelling at you is a great time not to listen and to make up limericks in your head.) Anyway, where was I? Oh yes, laugh and don't take people too seriously—and you'll be more compassionate.

You see, God loves you and wants you to love others and to love everybody. Try it. It's fun. If you need help, read Dr. Leo Buscaglia's books. He says, "Love deepens our sense of humor. It makes us capable of laughing at the world and human behavior, especially our own." Laughter and humor—somehow they make us more loving. So, from now, on live your life with love and laughter. That's how I sign my letters: "With love and laughter." Yes, I sign them in that way even when I write to Miss Manners.

So ... laugh. God will be so pleased. And it's great to please Him. So laugh a little. And remember, G. K. Chesterton said, "He who has the faith has the fun."

And another thing: when you pray to God—well, if you don't pray to God then you should start today—now stop interrupting me. When you pray, be cheerful, be humorous, be funny. Tell God jokes and funny stories. Don't be boring when you pray. Be funny. Now, don't tell me that God already knows the punch line. I know He does. But He wants to hear the joke from you, in your own words. He'll be touched that you *wanted* to tell Him a joke.

"He that is of a merry heart has a continual feast."
Proverbs 15:15

In the Middle Ages, jesters relaxed
by sitting on a wood pile.

The Middle Age Crisis

Of course, as a monk I'm interested in the Middle Ages. People often tell me, "You look so medieval," or "You're middle age! Just look at you!" People have certain ideas about the Middle Ages. People are stupid. Historians have certain ideas about the Middle Ages. Historians are more stupid. Hollywood filmmakers have certain ideas about the Middle Ages. Hollywood filmmakers are the most stupid. Here is what they all think:

Long ago, back in the Middle Ages, there lived a middle-aged man named Sid. He was an ignorant peasant who worked long hours at the local gruel factory, owned by the Lord of the Manor whose name was Ford Tanner. That's right, Ford Tanner was Lord of the Manor. His wife was named Sadie Tanner. She was the Lady of the Manor.

Sadie's brother was a monk of the local Monastery of St. Sanctimonious, who was the founder of the monastery and had named the monastery after himself. Sadie's brother was the Abbot, but his name was Costello. The monks were all very holy, but some of them had patches.

These monks were followers of Sactimonious who never

laughed, smiled or burped in his whole life. He prophesied the tragedy that one day, in an age far off, people would watch talk shows about problems—for entertainment!

Sactimonious had many followers, and both of them petitioned the Pope to make him a saint. The Pope wrote back and very kindly told them that he couldn't make him a saint while he was still alive. So these two followers decided to make him a saint on their own and they did so, following a self-help-how-to-book, and everything came out all right, except they put a little too much starch in the last rinse so Sanctimonious looked a little stiff. But nobody seemed to mind, and who cares anyway, because all the people then were ignorant peasants.

What really impressed the people was Sanctimonious' long beard. It was so long that he tripped over it constantly. So he finally folded it up and put it in a chest. That didn't help much because he kept tripping over the chest.

People came from all over the land to ask Sanctimonious his advice, questions and the time of day. Others came to ask him riddles and for a lift to the carnival in the next town. People lined up for days outside his door, happy to be able just to ask his door a question. All their problems they brought to him and insisted he give them a receipt. He ended quarrels, mended marriages and mended wagon wheels. Day and night people flocked to him. In the afternoon birds flocked to him. He was truly a wise man, a learned man. Though his vocabulary consisted of only four words, he used them well, considering the words were "Amen," "Sniffle," "Book" and "Microsoft."

People were so grateful to Sanctimonious that they brought him gifts, especially vegetables from their rotting surplus. Others brought toothpaste, hockey pucks and pretty, colored dirt. Some went all-out and brought spices, herbs and small islands. Others offered their services as gifts, offering to cut his hair, cut his lawn or cut his pay. Some offered to build him a new hermitage, but he refused, preferring to live with the other monks in their lovely revolving tower.

It seemed as though hundreds and thousands of people

visited Sanctimonious each day. Yet it was only a half dozen, but because they were so smelly it seemed like more.

Even Kings, Queens and Jacks would come to consult and insult Sanctimonious. It was rumored (according to "News of the Known World," which proved it with a drawing) that Sactimonious had been responsible for reconciling the Bantici Brothers, who hadn't spoken for 27 years after they had an argument over lasagna. They had argued over it for hours, then both had lost their balance and fallen into it. People took sides and one guy took someone's back. The brothers took numerous friends and relatives into each camp, where tents were allowed but not RV's.

Visiting Sactimonious became so popular that people made reservations years in advance and then forgot all about them. So everyone just mobbed the old man, right after his breakfast of porridge topped with marshmallows. They all crowded around him and shouted, "Long live Sanctimonious! May he live until the Renaissance!"

Even the great Queen Fritz came to see Santimonious. She patiently waited her turn for three seconds. Then she pulled Rank. Then she pushed Helen.

Queen Fritz asked Sanctimonious if she should marry the Duke of Dumbly, who had asked for her hand and hadn't returned it for weeks. Sanctimonious thought long and hard and had to be revived. Then he spoke slowly and asked, "Do you love him?"

"Well, sort of, but mostly it's because he promised to buy me a really cute pair of bobby socks."

"My child, most of the unhappiness in the world comes from wanting really cute pairs of bobby socks. My very own sister lost all her money in a bad bobby sock investment. She bought stock in a company that made bobby socks with little pictures of Mount Rushmore on them."

On hearing the name Mount Rushmore, Queen Fritz spit on the floor, threw the chair she was sitting on out the window, then quietly polished a few pieces of silver she carried with her for just such an occasion.

"No, my child," continued a recording of Sanctimonious (because he had fallen asleep), "don't be a duke and marry the dupe; I mean, anyway, your time's up, sister, so get out."

Queen Fritz thanked him and promised she'd name all her children after him, and her pets, plants, tennis racquets and her vegetables as well—everything, she would name after this holy man.

Anyway, Sid (remember him?) worked very hard at his job of making sure that the gruel had just the right amount of coriander to give it that proper gruel taste. Not that it mattered, because taste buds weren't discovered until 1782, by the Frenchman, Jul Yachild, whose wife was a sister of the Countess of Countless. She was the first countess to swim in the Danube on Tuesday evening after shopping at Wal-Mart for caramel popcorn.

But Sid cared about his work and wanted to be part of the team that made the world's best-tasting gruel, which was hard, because to be real gruel, it has to taste lousy. And a rival gruel company, that rented space in the same mud hut, began advertising that their gruel was the lousiest in all of Europe and the Totally Undiscovered New World, including Brooklyn. So there you have it. And now that you have it, could you please give it back?

After work, Sid walked back to town, passing through one of the town gates. It was on these impressive gates that shopkeepers would post notices telling people what they owed for their various purchases. They called these "Bill Gates."

As Sid walked down the crowded, filthy streets, teeming with vendors, street musicians and ballet-dancing camels, he amused himself by laughing at two runaway gargoyles who were playing Frisbee.

Sid continued his walk home and, at last, was at his very own house: a three-story, gabled mud hut. Once at home, his wife Crud (that's short for Crudmuda), lovingly greeted him at the door with the words, "Idiot! You forgot to pick up the dry cleaning again!" Which, of course, was her way of saying, "Uncle Seymour has fleas."

As soon as Sid was in his humble abode he would run out of it and go into his house. Once there, he would relax by the fire, wishing it was lit. He sat there, drinking his mead out of his cupped hands. (Cups weren't invented until two years later by a third cousin of Sid.) Then his children would gather round him and say, "Father, please tell us a story as we patiently await mother's loving preparation of our evening collation of gruel, and mud pies for dessert." (Made with real mud.)

So Sid would tell his children a story about the people who came to their town when he was a boy. They had come from far away; in fact, they had come from the future and were so excited to be back in the Middle Ages. They asked all kinds of questions and wanted only very typical medieval answers. They were very, very disappointed when they learned that some people could read, some people took a bath now and then and not everyone stuffed their mouths with food and ale and laughed at the kings jokes all at the same time. They were especially angry that the people didn't all wrap their heads in rags as they had seen in paintings.

These visitors pleaded with the peasants to be a drunken, useless bunch of morons with one chosen (by secret vote and a recommendation from a tamed wild boar) to be the Official Village Idiot. These people were so disappointed that they canceled their plans to take a few people to the future to help at the Medieval Theme Park in Atlantic City. Instead, they ran for Congress, jogged for the Senate and did high jumps for the President.

The children loved to hear this story, even though they had heard it before; as their memory span was only half that of their father's, they could remember the story for only ten minutes. Then the whole family sat down at the table to eat their gruel, which was very messy, as bowls hadn't been invented yet. (The same cousin invented them three years later.)

After supper the children did their homework, which was amazing, since they didn't go to school and no one gave them homework. Then they did their evening chores, such as making candles, shoeing horses and feeding their head lice. Then all the children went to sleep on the dining room table. Their mother lovingly covered them with a thick layer of dust.

Then Sid's wife put out the candles, setting them just outside the door so thieves wouldn't wake anyone if they wanted to steal them. Then she brushed her hair 100 times, took off her wig and removed her earrings, nose ring and the telephone ring. She then covered her face with an herbal mixture that the local witch told her (and sold her) would nicely age her face, giving her that coveted mature look that was all the rage according "Spring Vogue 1202." Then she put out the cat, seven rats and a bat.

Before bed, Sid always said his prayers, asking that he'd win the lottery and become king of the land, the name of which he didn't know, as maps weren't invented yet. (Four years later, a sister of that cousin invented them.) To help him sleep, Sid had half a sip of mango juice and then clubbed himself over the head. Then he went to sleep and dreamed about dragons and knights and Windows 98.

When Sid awoke, he had a quick breakfast of seventeen pounds of raw carrots and three toaster pastries burned on the fire. Then he walked to work, where he put in another grueling day. That's how life was back in the Middle Ages before deodorant and mouthwash, according to historians who don't know anything because they weren't there.

"Well, as I see it, funniness is an embellishment to life."
Robert Makinson

Let's live our lives with Love and Laughter!

Humor Makes Us Nice

We all want to be nice, don't we? We want to be good and kind. We also want to be thrifty, trustworthy, brave and famous. Now, there are several ways we can do this. We can read Miss Manners or we can act like Martha Stewart. Or, if we are wealthy, we can hire someone to be nice for us. But one really good way to help ourselves be nice is to use humor. By having a really great sense of humor, by seeing the funny in situations and by being funny, we can be nice.

Life gives us situations where we get impatient, angry, frustrated and covered with prickly heat. Instead of getting all worked up with impatience, anger and frustration, not to mention tension, stress and acne—let's be funny. Instead of giving in to negative emotions that hurt our health, let's turn to humor. Here's what I mean.

Take impatience. People, situations, having to wait (and especially the government) can make us feel impatient. If, at the moment, we feel impatience coming on, we can either jump into a swimming pool or laugh. Either way, we'll conquer our impatience. We need just to tell ourselves that, yes, something is happening here that we don't like, but we're going to try to see if there is anything funny going on that we can laugh about. Or, if we are dealing with others, let's say something funny rather than say something impatient.

Once I was left on the phone for a fifteen-minute wait. When someone finally picked up the phone, I said, "No problem, it gave me a chance to read *War and Peace*." That helped me to keep my cool and helped me to refrain from saying something like, "You left me here for fifteen minutes! I don't see why they let you be the President of the United States!"

I try to be patient but it isn't easy, because I hate waiting. Once, I learned my lesson though. What lesson it was, I am still trying to figure out. Once upon a time, on a dark, stormy night when I was in the seminary in Ireland, the Bishop asked me and another seminarian to write a skit for the 73rd anniversary of the school. Imagine, we had all been there seventy-three days.

Anyway, the other seminarian, whom I'll call Jack, but his name was Charles, and I went out to a cottage that the seminary owned. It was miles away from nowhere, on the edge of a river, a moor and the edge of my nerves. It was quiet and peaceful, a veritable writer's hideaway; in fact, over the door a sign read, "A Veritable Writer's Hideaway." We were busy at work there, writing and writing, when all of a sudden Jack said, "I'm going back to the school and get some pens and paper. You're wrong, we can't remember all of this."

So off he went, taking the car and leaving me there all alone. I waited and waited. The only thing I had to read was an old, moldy book entitled, "The Complete Book of Bishops Whose Middle Name Was Sven." It wasn't very enjoyable. The movie was better. So I threw the book against the wall and then, for fun, I threw the wall against the book. Then I sat there staring at the wallpaper, trying to count the petals on each of the roses. Hours later, I realized they were carnations. There I sat, impatiently fuming, with my back to the door.

When the door finally opened, I said with considerable contempt and without bothering to turn around, "You are the biggest idiot, moron, imbecile, rotten stupido in the world!" And I heard a voice respond, "Yes, but they let me be Bishop anyway." This incident was, I realize now, due to not using humor in dealing with impatience.

Anger is a big problem these days. Many people get very angry. And they express their angry freely. Now this isn't a very pleasant experience for all concerned. The person who gets angry is harming his or her health. More and more, research is telling us that anger and other negative emotions are harmful to our health and have bad effects on our immune system. Instead of getting angry we should get funny. There's a great book that I really like, and may even read someday, called, *Don't Get Mad; Get Funny!* It's written by Leigh Anne Jasheway and is published by Whole Person Associates. Leigh writes the syndicated column, "Laugh Lines," and is a consultant for a variety of corporations and lectures on topics related to wellness. She is also a standup comedienne and a stress management expert. In her book there is some really good advice—not like the drivel you find in this book. So let me quote—just try to stop me!

"Rather than feeling bad all over like you do when you get angry, the endorphins produced by the body during laughter provide natural painkillers, so you actually feel better. ... Laughter also 'massages' your internal organs. Besides feeling good, this massage can aid in digestion and improve the flow of blood and oxygen throughout the body. ... When you laugh you get better blood flow to all your major organs, including you brain. You can think more clearly, be more creative and solve problems better." Now, reread that last bit. If we get to laughing we can think more clearly and be more creative and therefore solve problems better! All this is very helpful when we are in situations where we are getting angry.

But the question is, how do you laugh when you feel like screaming? First, we have to realize that part of our angry feeling is just a desire to say something, to let off steam, to prevent ourselves from exploding.

Often people just say the first angry thing that comes into

their head. Something like, "You absolute moron! Why, I bet studies have shown that you are the sole cause of talk radio." How often I've heard that, particularly at the grocery store, Kmart and exclusive clubs in New York and London. Or, sometimes people holler, "Now, just a minute, buddy," and everyone has to stand around waiting for sixty seconds. Or, how often you've heard people so angry they can hardly speak say, "I'm so angry I can hardly speak." But what I think is going on here is just a person's need to say something. So I suggest saying something funny. Yes, say it to the person or machine you are angry with. No, not an insult that is supposed to be funny, but say something really funny.

If someone cuts you off while driving, you could holler, "If you do that again I'll sing an aria from Madame Butterfly."

If someone gets in front of you in line at the drivethru dentist, say cheerfully, "I'm honored to have you in line in front of me and now we can discuss the value of reading travel books about Turkey rather than Norwegian novels about ants."

If someone is downright rude to you, just say, "Now, I'm sure you really think I'm perfect, wonderful and the greatest person who has ever lived, with the possible exception of the man who invented glass tires."

Actually, you can probably think of better funny things than these. I'm sure you can't think of stupider things, though.

It's really important to conquer our anger. (Controlling it isn't enough.) I know from experience—not my own, but because of my Uncle Stanley. He lives in Cleveland. Now, Uncle Nle (oh, by the way, we call him Nle as a short form of Stanley) really gets angry, mad and has a temper that he lost years ago and has never been able to find. Once, his wife bought him a shirt. It was a nice shirt with pretty red, green, pink, mauve and burgundy colored flowers, all made up to look like square dancers riding hot air balloons. You know the kind.

Anyway, Uncle Nle opened the package, took out the shirt, smelled it, and then his rapturous joy left him when he noticed that there were large holes in both underarms of the shirt, the pockets were sewn shut and the collar had been shredded. (His wife, my Aunt Twapsie, is a compulsive shopper, who doesn't open her eyes much.) Uncle Nle was angry, furious and rather mad. He stuffed the shirt in the store's bag and rushed over to the store. In his anger he forgot the car and ran all the way there. His wife followed with the car but couldn't find a parking place, so she went back home, packed her things and left to join a convent.

Uncle Nle stormed into Sears with the shirt and went up to the "Nonjudgmental Center for Purchase Reversal," the new politically correct term for "Returns." Uncle Nle pushed aside the people who were waiting in line. Fortunately, all fifty-eight of them were peace-loving folk, or decided they didn't want to return anything anyway, because no one got rough with him. He began by hollering, "Hey, you stupid, blonde, high school dropout, I want to return this shirt that your lousy, crummy store sold my wife, who, granted, isn't an intellectual genius or a connoisseur of belle lettres, but you guys have some nerve taking advantage of her and selling her a shirt that looks like it has suffered by being on the Maury Povich show. I demand you take it back and give me a full cash refund."

"I'm sorry, sir, but we can't take back that shirt."

"What are you saying? Why of all the low down, slow down and show down, let's look up and then look down, rotten things! I demand that you take back this shirt."

"I'm sorry sir, but we can't."

"All right, I've been pleasant and ever so sweet about this, but now you've really got me just a teensy weensy bit annoyed, and I'm not going to tolerate your insubordination to a commanding officer, a tax payer and a member of the Bald Men of America Club. I insist and demand you take back this shirt."

"No, sir. I'm sorry but I can't do that."

This was too much for Uncle Nle. He grabbed the clerk's ears and yanked on them. Then he grabbed his nose and yanked on it. Then he grabbed a tuba from the music department and played the "William Tell Overture." Then he jumped on the counter and stomped on the little memo pad that read, "A Cutesy Little Messagepoo While You Were Learning Tractor Trailer Repair." Then he slowly jumped off the counter and screamed again, "I demand you take back this shirt."

Now, this girl was smart. Before she tried to say something this time she stuffed the stomped-on memo pad in Uncle Nle's mouth until he couldn't respond and said, "I can't take it back," as she held up the bag, "It's from J. C. Penny's." There is a great lesson from this story, but I have no idea what it is.

Getting back to the book, *Don't get Mad, Get Funny*: Leigh Anne Jasheway makes an interesting point when she teaches that laughter helps people to trust you. Now, in a tense or angry situation, trust is a great help. If you can get people to trust you, well, they might not agree with you completely, but at least they will listen and believe you are good, honest, sincere and use deodorant.

Then there are times when we aren't so much angry as frustrated. As we all know, the word frustrated come from the Latin *frustratium*, which means "to sit at the opera on a very hot night and sweat profusely." So much for root meanings. When we are frustrated, humor and laughter and a change of clothes are great helps.

You might be surprised to read this, but I am often frustrated. In the last ten minutes I've been frustrated twenty-eight times. You see, I'm typing this on a computer, and machines get me tense, angry and frustrated. It's because we don't think alike. Oh, machines don't think? Maybe that's my problem. Anyway, I get frustrated with this stupid computer because it won't cooperate. It makes me type everything into it. Anyway, when you are frustrated with, say, a human being (just for the sake of argument), rather than let the frustration grow, and rather than saying things you will regret two minutes later, try saying something like the following:

"My dear, if you don't hurry up and stop telling me that I

need form A78 in order to exchange this collar for my pet rhino, we are all going to be a wee bit late for our afternoon tea, aren't we?"

"Yes, librarian, I did put this book through the paper shredder instead of the photocopy machine, but, really, life is too short to worry about such things and a hundred years from now who will care and we must gather roses while we may and stop and smell the sunsets."

"I'm not trying to rush you or the mechanic, but you did imply that my car would be ready before I made all the payments on it."

"Of course, I'm not upset. I never liked that priceless painting anyway, and I do understand your urgent need for something to put under your car when you changed the oil. I can get another Picasso."

"Me frustrated? No, I'm just a bit hungry, so I thought I'd just sit here quietly and chew on my lapels."

Yes, the best way to handle impatience, anger and frustration is to be funny. Try it and let me know how you do. I'm sure you will find that it will give greater joy, happiness and aerodynamics to your life. I just know it will help you so much that you will insist on sending a large donation to our monastery and will promise to name all your children Craig or at least Giarc, which is Fritz spelled sideways.

And so, that concludes another adventure in this most amazing book, and, until next time, we would like to thank you for being with us today, and from all of us here to all of you there, we want to say that we are here and you are there, and that is neither here nor there. This has been rehearsed before a live (but bored) audience.

"If we do not choose to look for humor, believe me, it will look for us."
Liz Curtis Higgs

Put on a funny constume and stand in a tree.
It's funny. Try it at parties.

So What's Funny?

Having a sense of humor and being funny are not the same thing. See how I get to the point? A person could have a sense, or awareness, of what is funny and not have the gift or talent of being funny. Having a sense of humor, seeing the silly or the ridiculous, is a great help in life. G. K. Chesterton wrote, "The man who sees the consistency in things is a wit; the man who sees the inconsistency in things is a humorist." Being funny is an added benefit. Both are gifts; both can be developed. Both refer to humorousness, or to what is funny. But what is "funny"? It seems that "funny" involves one or more of the following:

— surprise
— exaggeration
— insight.

Surprise is the essence of the method of the standup comic (or the politician). First, a more or less serious line is given. This is called the "setup." Then the pause—followed by the unexpected. This is used also with many humorous plays or television shows. This type of humor uses mainly words, dialogue, rather than funny situations, which the older comedy movies and television shows, such as "I Love Lucy," used. Some feel that there has been, lately, too much emphasis on word-humor and not enough on funny actions. It does seem to be true that bigger laughs more often come from action humor, as when Groucho Marx put fifteen people in his tiny stateroom on a ship in "A Night at the Opera."

But getting back to surprise. The standup comic surprises us, after pausing. A talented comic uses what is called "comic timing," as does the comic actor. This timing is the most important part of the act. Milton Berle said that once he got the audience laughing, he could say anything, if he timed it correctly, and they'd laugh. Timing is the thing. Timing sets us up for the surprise of the punch line. The fact that we are expecting to be surprised as we listen to a comedian doesn't seem to take away from the surprise.

Much of the laughter a comedian stimulates derives from people's expectation of hearing something funny. There they are, sitting in an audience or watching TV, expecting to laugh. Seems like a lot of expecting for people who are repeatedly surprised by the punch line! But it works. What happens is that, while the audience expects to be surprised, they are truly surprised by what the surprise is. Did you follow that? The surprise is not that the comedian said something funny, but what funny thing he said.

Part of the secret of getting laughs is the audience mentality that develops when a group of people sit together and watch an act. (How many people does it take to be an audience? Nobody knows really. Probably more than one.) An audience will find truly funny, and laugh at, things that, as individuals, they might think are only slightly amusing or not funny at all.

Another factor is important—room temperature. The cooler the room, the more people will laugh. Just let the air conditioning break down in Las Vegas on a hot night! That poor standup comic will get very few laughs—even if he has an audience.

Here is an example. I once spoke at a Catholic conference in Seattle. Though, as in this case, the subject matter of the talk was not humorous, I always like to begin with something funny. It warms up the audience like nothing else (except giving them all sweaters). Not only do they listen better, they are also more receptive, more open to what the speaker is saying, and less apt to be engaged in Japanese paper folding, during the talk. But it's best for the speaker to say four or five sentences at the very beginning of the talk, that are not an attempt to be funny. It's nearly impossible to get people to laugh at the very, very beginning of a talk; they are focusing on the speaker, getting settled, etc., but are not ready to laugh. But after only a few introductory sentences they should be ready.

As an out-of-town speaker in Seattle, I began with two things that are nearly guaranteed to get a laugh: 1. Something funny about where I'm from. 2. Something funny about the city or state where the meeting is held. This "local humor" goes over real big if it is gentle and not insulting. So I began with something about my Boston accent and that I would need a translator. They liked that. Then I said that back East we do not know much about the great Northwest. (Which is true.) All we know, I told them, is that it rains a lot. "Before I left, fourteen people gave me umbrellas."

Doesn't seem very funny now, and it was a total exaggeration, but the Seattle audience loved it. It was very local humor. Then, still referring to our lack of knowledge in the East of the great Northwest (which I was exaggerating), I said that when I told a friend of mine I was going to Washington, she said, "That's nice. You'll get to see the White House." They really liked it. That was surprise working.

Please note that although this was "local humor," the brunt of the jokes was not the locals but the east coast people who, I being one, could be joked about. (For some reason, it's okay to tell Irish jokes if you're Irish.) Then I used a bit of "research" I had done. The day before, I had learned that the Seattle baseball team is called the "Mariners." (I'd never heard of them.) Continuing the theme of east coast "ignorance" (which was really my baseball ignorance), I said, "You know, until yesterday, I always thought the 'Mariners' were a labor union." Big laugh. Applause. They loved it.

Yes, much of their appreciation was because it was local. And I did try to do my best with comic timing—those pauses. But to be honest, most of the laughter came from audience mentality. Had I done all those lines to all those people individually, there might have been some laughter but it would not have been as much.

Now, in the above examples there was also exaggeration. Surely some people in the East know a great deal about the Northwest. But many don't. About all I know is that it rains. So there is truth here. It was Phyllis Diller, the talented standup comedienne, who said that humor, though exaggerated, must be based on truth. Exaggerate it like crazy, Phyllis said, but base it on truth. It might be funny if I said that I ate a light lunch and for dessert had—two whole cheesecakes. It wouldn't be funny if I said I ate 40,000 cheesecakes. It's too unreal.

Perhaps we don't often think of this, but really funny things are exaggerations based on truth. Steve Allen said, "Nothing is quite as funny as the unintended humor of reality." And Steven Leacock wrote, "Humor may be defined as the kindly contemplation of the incongruities of life and the artistic expression thereof." And George Bernard Shaw said, "My way of joking is to tell the truth; it's the funniest joke in the world." And that great comic genius and the funniest man ever, Sid Caesar, said, "Comedy has to be truth. You take the truth and you put a little curlicue at the end."

Humor, at times, can also involve insights, sometimes brilliant insights. Here's an interesting thought from M. Dale Baughman: "A comedian's job is to make people laugh. But a humorist makes them laugh and then think. Humor is a way of life, a pattern of behaving. It's the ability to bend without breaking." Humor can teach a lesson. It can enlighten, gently prod people about prejudice or erroneous ways. This kind of humor is usually not the type that gets big laughs. Hopefully, it gets big results. Sometimes this kind of humor doesn't get any laughs at all but a point is made. Humor should serve in this way, too. Satire is humor serving a very important purpose—to try to make the world a better place.

Animal Farm, George Orwell's novel about the evils of Communism, is a satire. All the animals take over the farm. They do things collectively, for "all are equal." But then, the pigs start to run everything. When other animals complain of this, the pigs respond that although all the animals are equal, they, the pigs, are "more equal." That's a brilliant line.

Humor can wake people up and make them think. William Zinsser, a great teacher of writing and the author of several books on writing, explains, "What I want to do is to make people laugh so that they'll see things seriously."

A good example of using humor to teach is Mark Twain's book *Huckleberry Finn*. The part where Huck accepts doing a "terrible wrong"; that is, helping Jim escape from slavery, is very clever. We, the readers, know that it isn't wrong, that it's very right, and we also know that Mark Twain knows it! But carefully, thoughtfully, Huck decides to do this wrong thing. That is humor, teaching.

Though there was much to find fault with in the television show "All in the Family," the main point of the show, though often missed, was a very good one. We laughed at Archie Bunker's bigoted opinions. We laughed because they were stupid; they were incorrect. Perhaps a prejudiced person did learn a lesson.

There are kinds of "humor" that don't deserve the name. Laughing at people, the put-down, the insult, the sarcastic wisecrack are not real humor and are not funny. As Dorothy Parker wrote, "Wit has truth in it; wisecracking is simply calisthenics with words." Vulgarity, also isn't funny. Red Skelton said that people laugh at vulgar jokes because they are embarrassed. The laughter is really just a nervous twitter. Comics who do vulgar jokes aren't talented enough to get laughs without these jokes— or rather, they are, but they don't realize it.

Oh, that's funny! Let me get it down!

Writing Funnily

Remember I told you a while back that you should try to be funny to bring more joy, happiness and laughter into the lives of others—well, in this chapter I want to tell you about humorous writing. It was Dorothy Parker who said that it "is a strange force that compels a writer to be a humorist." Now, we've got that out of the way. You may not think of yourself as a writer. You may not even think of me as a writer. You may not even think, for all I know. I certainly don't. But you might want to write something funny in order to cheer people up; a great and glorious thing to do. You might write a letter, an article, a book, an encyclopedia or instructions for assembling a one-piece "crash-o-matic" vegetable smasher.

By the way, as I'm writing this I'm sitting on the veranda of the Zolixi Motel overlooking highway I-90 in Arkansas. I'm not really. But haven't you noticed that writers often tell you where they are when they're writing? Personally, I've never noticed that. But to get to the point of our topic—how to write funny. I have frequently been asked how I write funny, and also why. But let's forget that second part. How to write funny? I always wonder what I should answer. Some possible answers are:

— I'm a genius. Writers of genius don't know how they write; they just write.

— I read other peoples' funny books and make slight changes. (Like the name of the author.)

— I'm really trying to write serious; it's just my luck it comes out funny.

— I subscribe to "Funny Writers Non-Copyright Digest," a daily publication published by a subsidiary of Oz Oil Company.

How does one write funny? I really don't know. But I do have a friend who writes funny books. She writes three or four a year. So I called her and the phone conversation went like this:

"How are you?"
"Who is it?"
"It's me, Brother Craig."
"Did you call collect?"
"No, of course not. It's a local call."
"Do you want a loan?"
"No, just to ask you a few questions."
"Okay, go ahead."
"How do you write so funny?

After a long pause, during which she flossed her teeth, she said, "Well, Brother, it's like this. I sit down at the typewriter, and I start the first sentence having no idea how that sentence will end or what I'm going to say. It's the same with all the sentences in the book. If I began a sentence having any idea how it would end or what I was going to say it might make sense and then wouldn't be funny. Goodbye."

This friend isn't much for small talk. But thinking over her profound advice, I realized I write the same way. Don't you agree? But seriously, weren't there any good books you could have chosen—why are you reading this one?

Anyway, I once was asked to write an autobiographical article on what it is like to be an author (me) who has been nominated for the Nobel Prize for literature. The fact that I had nominated myself didn't seem to matter to the editor of the "Linzdotterly Literary Quarterly Review." I share with you only the first paragraph due to international copyright and embarrassment.

"As a nominee for the Nobel Prize in literature I must say that I am not only deeply honored to be (as aforesaid) a Nobel nominee but to have the additional honor, distinction and grandeur of being nominated by such a distinguished, charming, cultured, intelligent, noble, regal, sophisticated author as myself only adds to my esteem, gratitude and appreciation for the Nobel Prize itself (and the money) and therefore I hereby and forthwith accept the nomination (and the money) hoping that all the greatest writers in the world will decline along with everyone else or else I won't win (and the money) and truly, in conclusion, let me sincerely add that, however little or much I have written, and however great my other civic activities have been, both in my hometown and on the international level—particularly for the restoration of "Happy Holiday Picnic Park" in Ridge Ranch, Virginia—and other notable activities for which I am duly noted—I must sincerely add that if I win the prize (and the money) I have, most truthfully, to say that I have perhaps one distinction, one great contribution to the noble art of letters (that means literature), and that is, as you perhaps have realized, I, Brother Craig, the Nobel Prize nominee have (all by myself) written just now what seems to be the world's longest sentence—so I SHOULD win the prize."

Let us now consider humor as therapy. (Surprise. I just changed the subject, and you can't stop me!) By humor and laughter, especially when we laugh with (not at) ourselves and the silly things we do, we take ourselves out of the center. We finally admit that the whole world does not revolve around "me."

Take for example my cooking. I love to cook, though my friends hate it. I am, you will no doubt be surprised to learn, not a terrible cook. I am worse! I'm overly creative. I once made a noodle-apple-cinnamon sandwich. One of my favorite recipes is vinegar-peanut-butter cookies. I believe that cooking is an art: abstract. Here's a great recipe for company which I call Tuesday Night Surprise:

1 bottle of molasses
12 oz. dried black olives
200 pounds of rice
A pinch of salt
1 container of maraschino cherries
4 cups of applesauce

Mix together in cement mixer. Bake on medium low for two minutes. Serve hot. Leave town.

My real specialty regarding cooking is speed:

Breakfast — one minute.
Lunch — two and a half minutes.
Supper — (for twelve people) five minutes.

I will share my secret. I use every pot, pan and spoon in the house. Cleanup takes several hours, with professional help.

I really love to cook, because then I can be creative. Like writing! But I'm afraid my food is funnier than my writing. Friends lately have been asking me to *their* house to eat, or to restaurants. I wonder why. I always offer to do the cooking.

Once I had a dinner party at the monastery and served the following (feel free to use this menu, but please don't give my name):

Pineapple-lemon soup
Graham crackers
Horseradish as the main course
Carrots a la pepper
Potatoes carefully burned
Dessert: onion flavored tofu with a mocha sauce.

Cooking can be fun. It can be funny. Eating out can be funny. Once, at a local diner, I was the eight billionth customer —and got one dill pickle free, IF I ordered the pasta plate special. I have eaten in restaurants in the United States, Europe, South America and Asia. My absolute favorite is, sorry to say, my own cooking. Please pass the ketchup for my orange juice.

*And if you call before midnight tonight you'll receive—
well, we'll see what we can find for you.*

Scams

I'm surprised Moses wasn't given an eleventh commandment: "Thou shalt not be stupid." People are really silly when it comes to believing stupid things. At least I am. Anyway, by now you, no doubt, have either stopped reading this book or consider me a wise and learned sage, a veritable monk-on-a-mountain-top awaiting the questions of determined seekers as to the meaning of life, lottery numbers and why we say, "run it under cold water" when we mean "put it under cold running water." So I'm sure, at this point, you'd like my opinion on that deeply philosophical subject—as seen on "Lulu Lupple's Local Cable Community Call-in Show"—the truth and falsehood of scams.

My friend Danny used to say I was, well, kind of gullible. Of course, it's not true. I mean, just because I fell for the following ads in the back of magazines (they all had P.O. Boxes in Florida) doesn't mean I'm gullible.

— Language pens. You write in English and it comes out in the language of your choice. Available in Spanish, French, German, Italian and Sanskrit.

— Royal titles. Completely genuine. King, Queen, Prince, Princess, Duke, Duchess, Earl, Earless—order them all at our special price.

— A Ph.D. without any study. All subjects available (including pedicurist).

— Prime land in Tierra del Fuego. No money down. Free plot plan, map and sun hat.

— Earn billions of dollars each week with our instructions on how to turn ordinary household items (e.g., a toaster) into solid gold. The American Alchemy Academy. Guaranteed.

— Stop aging. Completely tested and safe. You'll never age. Immortality guaranteed.

— Our special pill stops hair loss, melts away pounds and gives you a Yiddish accent.

— Learn to fly like Peter Pan. (No airplane required.) Eight easy lessons on video.

— Learn fluent Chinese, Mongolian, Tibetan and Hong Kong slang in one evening.

— Meet famous Hollywood stars. They'll be begging you to attend their parties.

— Find oil in your backyard. It's easy and fun. No drilling necessary.

— We'll publish your book, make it into a movie and pay you big bucks.

— 200,000,000 free kumquat recipes. Order before December 15 and we'll include a free topographical map of Indiana.

— Trace your family tree back 8,000 years. It's easy. It's fun. Impress your friends.

— Learn cake decorating, airport tower control and weight lifting without study.

— Become another person, literally. You can be anyone you wish. Our special techniques can transform you into Donald Trump, Queen Elizabeth, Howdy Doody, etc. Millions of people available. Completely safe.

— Learn the secret of the Aztecs, Herbert Hoover's mother's middle name and water skiing over the telephone.

— Our speed reading course can teach you to read eight million paragraphs per minute.

So does that make me gullible? You should have seen the ones I didn't respond to—now they were unbelievable!

"Does God have a sense of humor? He must have if He created us."
Jackie Gleason

*Doing a ballet with a frog can relieve
stress and tension.*

Let's Stress Humor

Stress and tension are the most common complaints these days. Okay, the most common complaint is—you can't get a cab and then when you get one the driver doesn't speak English and can't find the Center for Reluctant Raisins. Anyway, stress and tension are a big problem. A report to the President's Science Advisor places the cost of stress to the economy at $200 billion annually.

Why are people tense and stressed out? It's simple—they waste time watching TV, and then don't have time to do all they need to do. "But I watch TV to relax," they whine. "Silence, knave!" I respond. Okay, now you know the cause of stress and tension.

The question now is—does humor help reduce stress and tension? By the way, I don't believe in stress management. Stress isn't something nice like time or money that should be managed. It's something nasty that should be eliminated. Where was I? Oh yes, the question—can humor reduce stress and tension?

The answer is Yes. You knew that was the answer. Why do writers do this? Why do we go on and on, blah, blah, blah, writing things that everybody knows and charging money for books that really could just be done on some index cards—a few helpful hints. Anyway, now that I'm stuck in this chapter—hey, you can read another chapter or go trim the shrubs or do something useful like join a civic earth-friendly group dedicated to that cause of causes—to Save the Marzipan.

To save the Marzipan! What a noble work! You could picket, write to your congressman, send letters to editors and editors to letters. You could wear recycled, bio-organic T-shirts which read, "Help the Ecosphere! Save the Marzipan!" Or, you could attend a conference and listen to speakers wearing earth-friendly shoes that only cause "cushioned contact" with the earth, our home, our mother, our place to hang out, man. These speakers would enlighten you on "Marzipan and The Ozone Layer," "Marzipan—Who Will remember?" "Marzipan, Global Warming and Postcards of the Tito Theme Park in Zagreb," "Marizpan: Our Children's World, a Legacy" and "The Cycle of Life and Marzipan's Role in Sustainable Rain Forest Mopping Up." And—wait, where was I? Oh yes, tension and stress. Well, I think it's time to quote some people whose IQ is greater than mine. Not ALL of them—there isn't room.

Way back in the last century when they didn't have computers, a guy who was some kind of philosopher or something, Herbert Spencer (whose mother called him Herbie Spencie no doubt) said that laughter is a mechanism for relieving excess tension. So there you have it. But, wait a minute! "Excess" tension! I don't want *any!*

John Morreall, Ph.D., director of Humorworks (which is a registered trademark, but I don't know how to do one of those little r's with a circle around it). Anyway, he is also the author of *Taking Laughter Seriously* (State University of New York Press). He writes, "The person who has a sense of humor is not just more relaxed in the face of a potentially stressful situation, but is more flexible in his approach. Even when there is not a lot going on in his environment, his imagination and innovativeness will help keep him out of a mental rut, will allow him to enjoy himself and so will prevent boredom and depression."

Viktor Frankl, who knew something far worse than stress and tension, in a concentration camp, wrote, "I never would have made it if I could not have laughed. It lifted me momentarily out of this horrible situation, just enough to make it livable."

Lisa Rosenberg, psychologist and nurse at Chicago's Rush-Presbyterian-St. Luke's Medical Center, tells us, "Humor is not just about laughing at a joke. It is a perspective about life. It's an emotional release, and it also allows you to continue to function in stressful situations. One of the most important aspects of using humor as a stress buster is one's ability to produce it spontaneously. That's really the key to the wonderful effects of humor, to using it as a coping strategy."

Okay, so it's time for me to put my two cents in. When you are tense, have lots of stress—what funny stuff should you do?

—Talk with a Yiddish accent.

—Sing songs while impersonating Groucho Marx.

—Form a conga line all alone and dance around the room.

—Laugh at the petty things you let bother you. Just throw you head back and laugh and think of the day in the not-too-distant future when you'll be a rich and famous rock star.

—Tell yourself that stress and tension lead to serious sickness and start laughing.

—Throw out your trouble! Come on—get happy!

—Laugh at life's little difficulties and proceed to achieve your greatest dream: playing the violin in a Romanian Gypsy band.

—Laugh at absolutely nothing and for no reason whatsoever, and it will get rid of the stress and tension. So do it! Now!

Another way humor can help get rid of stress and tension is through gentle laughter at how seriously we take things. I mean, we're forever making mountains out of molehills and molehills out of anthills and anthills out of—well, you get the idea. Why do we do it? I mean, why do we get so worried, worked and concerned about issues that we won't even remember next week? Petty things, small annoyances and disagreements—we blow them out of all proportion, and we get tense and all stressed.

So instead, let's laugh at how we make trivia into major issues, and let's laugh until we stop doing it!!! We're making ourselves sick and making everyone around us sick with worry, high-strung nerves and tension. We are killing ourselves! So let's just stop. You stop it! Do you hear me? Stop it right now. Start enjoying life, start laughing, having fun and looking at life with humor. Somewhere in this book I think I've quoted someone who said humor is "a defense mechanism against the universe." Well, humor and being funny are surely good defense mechanisms against stress and tension.

How? Well, just start acting. Get ready to win an Academy Award. What I mean is *act*—fake it, pretend. Force yourself to be funny—to say funny things, to do funny things when you are stressed-out or tense or when you're in stressful or tense situations—and you'll see results! Well, you may not see all the stress and tension go away instantly but you will see them lessen. The more you are funny, or the more time and effort you put into being funny, the better the results.

Another reason humor is such a good weapon against stress and tension is that it helps us to feel more "in control." In a stressful situation, we feel that we are definitely NOT in control, and that the rotten, lousy situation is controlling us. Humor helps a lot, because when you do something funny you are deciding, you are doing something you've chosen to do—you're in control.

This feeling of control is even greater if there are people around, and they laugh at whatever funny thing you do or say. Making people laugh gives you a fun feeling of innocent control and power. When I give my humor talks, it's amazing, the feeling of control, to look out at the audience and think: after two more lines or sentences that I am going to say, they will laugh—I will *make* them laugh. It's awesome.

It gives me such a nice warm feeling of absolute power that I have decided that I simply must take over the world! And I will do it! Do you hear me? I will! And don't forget that Ralph Waldo Emerson said, "If you want to take over the world you've got to keep it amused." Don't forget that!

So I, the Mirthful Monk WILL take over the world! No one can stop me! I shall be the leader of all! I shall be the super-duper "dominance facilitator" (the new term for dictator). I shall take over the world and, more importantly, I shall declare myself King of Boca Raton!!! But still, even after I've taken over the world (probably late next week—I'm busy with a book signing on Monday), I must not take myself too seriously. That's a really terrible mistake of many dominance facilitators. I mean, what good would it do me to take over the world if I become stressed and tense and forgot all about humor!?!

I would have made this chapter longer but the publisher wants to get this book out soon, so I have only a few days left to finish and I have a dentist appointment on Thursday and a rabbi friend is visiting tomorrow so I'm really pressed for time which is why I am so stressed out and have so much tension. I mean, I've been working on this *day* after *day*— and I *really* can't take the stress *any more* ...

"What is funny about us is precisely that we take ourselves too seriously."
Reinhold Neibuhr

The only thing I've ever won is balloons.

Game Shows

Watching game shows is, of course, a sign that one's life is completely meaningless. Of course, I only watch them to do research. Then again, doing research means one's life is completely meaningless.

Don't you just love those game shows? My favorite is "The Price is Wrong," with Bobby Boyish as the host. Bobby says something like—

"As all of our daily viewers (that is, bored housewives) know, the object of our game is to guess the wrong price of each product. Our contestants today are Mr. Poindexter and Miss Esmerelda O'Reilly-Jones-Smith-Dugginham. Are you ready? Good. This first product—one match from a book of matches from a box of fifty books. Mr. Poindexter?"

"One-eighth of a penny."

"Correct! You lose. Miss O'Reilly-Jones-Smith-Dugginham?"

"$875."

"Wrong! You win!"

"Now, our Ed McMahon look-alike, with the John Forsythe voice, will tell you what you've won."

"An all-expense-paid trip to the Ohio River Valley for six months."

She screams, cries and hugs and kisses the podium.

"Our next product. This pocket TV with a VCR. It has color options and can be plugged into a cigarette lighter and sometimes makes coffee. Mr. Poindexter?"

"$375."

"Correct. You lose. Now, Miss O'Reilly-Jones-Smith-Dugginham?"

"$8,750,400,820.13."

"Wrong! You win again! What does this lovely lady in the burlap and velvet suit win?"

"She gets the TV."

Winner screams, jumps up three times and down twice and files her fingernails.

"Our final product is this Toyota Volkswagen with an automatic toaster. Mr. Poindexter, try your worst."

"$16,782 plus tax."

"Exactly! You lose! Miss whatever-it-is?"

"Four cents"

"Wrong! You are our grand prize winner! Here's your prize!"

"A trip to Hawaii, seventeen marbles, an autographed photo of Kermit the Frog and a free tour of the White House."

Winner runs throughout the audience, jumps up and down and reads a book. Booby says, "All of our contestants, audience and crew will receive a box of instant rice, a trip to Disneyland, a supply of scrap paper and a broken calculator. Until tomorrow this is 'The Price is Wrong' and I'm still Bobby Boyish here in northern Maine with the Tampa Philharmonic Orchestra."

Game shows can be stupid. I've been on only one. It was the one where you have to lift weights under water. It's not because I lost that I'm against some game shows. It's just that I hate to see people who know who played the waiter in the original "Beau Geste" and who also know who ran for

President in 1996. I can't stand it. And also, the winners get so excited. Over what? Tons of money or a vacation and a new car or house or macaroni for life. Big deal. I don't even like macaroni.

One game show I do like is "Name the Idiot," where the contestants try to guess the occupation of the person wrapped in brown paper. Of course, the contestants are celebrities who can't find work. Their questions are profound:

"Does your work involve Philosophy?"
"Are you paid in pennies?"
"Can you whistle while you work?"
"Do you use your left brain, right brain or no brain?"

Usually they can guess the occupation. Some interesting occupations have been featured:

A man who does ice sculptures by licking the ice.

A lady who electric shocks hair to give it a permanent perm.

A guy who teaches Russian to microwaves.

A girl who does Rodney Dangerfield impersonations while decorating wedding cakes.

A man who runs a company that quickly changes tires while the car is moving.

One can really learn a lot from game shows. One can learn to hate TV. There is a really stupid game show where the contestants try to guess what the host is thinking. What makes it really absurd is that the host is allowed to lie. No one has ever won. The show has been on for thirteen years. Another show "Opinion Option" is where the person who has the stupidest opinion wins. Here are some of the winners:

— "I think the government would be greatly improved if politicians ate more lettuce."

— "I think that weathermen should not be allowed to decide the weather."

— "In my opinion, women who have red hair should not be allowed to vote, eat or paint window shutters."

— "The problem with this country is that the taxpayers have to pay taxes."

— "The solution to dirt, dust and mildew buildup inside your coffee pot is to scrub thoroughly with a Greek philosophy textbook."

— "Congress shouldn't allow anything."

— "People should not be allowed to waste time sleeping."

Another game show is one where people try to tell their life story the fastest. It must be a day-by -day account. I was amazed when a man 106 years old won. He told his life story in twenty seconds.

Why do people watch game shows? Why do people play games? Why do people ask questions like, "Name a state that begins with the letter U"? It's ridiculous. (The answer is Utah.)

"When a thing is funny, search it for a hidden truth."
George Bernard Shaw

Be sure never to wallpaper a window.

House Ugly

No doubt you're wondering why this book would include a chapter on interior decoration as featured in popular magazines. There are several philosophical, psychological, sociological, anthropological and very illogical reasons.

— To make the book longer (which is the only reason you'll believe).

— Because it would take a comic to live in the cluttered, ridiculous rooms that these magazines feature.

— Home is where the heart is and the heart has its reasons which reason knows nothing about.

— Every man's home is his castle.

— "Home for the Holidays," "Homeward Bound" and "Look Homeward Angel" all have something to do with homes as do homing pigeons, home plate and Sherlock Holmes.

— You can tell a lot about people by their wallpaper.

— To get this book mentioned on the "Home and Garden Channel."

— The publisher's third cousin owns a plastic rug company.

— I'm a member of an interior decorator's motorcycle club.

— To make the book longer.

I agree with Mary McBride, who said, "A thing of beauty is a chore forever." Of course, the cluttered look is in. Just look at any interior decorating magazine like "Lovely and Homey," or "Homes of the Snobbish and Ostentatious." Rooms stuffed with furniture, paintings and bric-a-brac give them the homey impression of an obstacle course. The living rooms have four couches, three antique chairs, fourteen throw rugs and a basketball hoop over the fireplace. Beds in bedrooms have at least sixty embroidered pillows, each one done by a different Hollywood celebrity's aunt. Kitchens are fantastic (literally). Pots and pans hang from the ceiling, baskets clutter the floor, and, along with a stove, there is a microwave, dishwasher, trash compactor and a jacuzzi for washing vegetables. And, of course, before the photos were taken, the kitchen was given that "lived-in look"—a dish towel carelessly thrown over a chair (with real wrinkles ironed in), a half-rolled-out pie crust and seventeen large pumpkins, cut in half. Children's bedrooms contain hundreds of stuffed toys, games, two books and an antique airport control tower. Patios have a swimming pool and fourteen large cement elephants.

My own apartment (before I became a monk) consisted of a kitchen, bedroom, dining room, library, study, conservatory, solarium, billiard room and gym. They were all in one room. I divided each of these activity centers by drawing yellow lines on the floor. I used mustard. I did my own interior decorating and achieved the look that might result from a collaboration between Ivana Trump with Phyllis Diller. I got that cozy-clutter look by not cleaning it.

The kitchen consisted of a sink, a microwave and a walk-in refrigerator. (The mice walked in all the time.) My bedroom was done in organdy and mauve—one sheet was organdy, the other was mauve. The dining room table was custom-made by stacking empty pizza boxes. The library consisted of one bookshelf, which contained only the entire works of William F. Buckley, Jr. The study next to the library had my desk, a computer and my collection of Norwegian remote controls. The conservatory had one plant that decoratively grew up the wall. Most people call it "mold."

My only window, I called the solarium. The view was breathtaking. That is, when the window was open, due to the pollution, it took your breath away. The billiard room had a toy ping-pong table and the gym had a treadmill (endorsed by Arthur Godfrey, Mel Blanc and Twiggy) which wasn't used much, except for holding empty Häagen-Dazs cartons.

When I had friends over, they always complained about (1) having to bring their own chair, (2) having to shovel out a space for it, (3) that I changed for the visit. Some friends offered to help me clean the place. One friend offered to burn it. Another friend gave me one of those self-help books (large print edition). It was, "How To Clean Your House in Just 18 Years." Then another friend loaned me a housework video, "How To Have Fun Doing Housework." It explained things like, "Mix one part vinegar, two parts boric acid, one part red wine and three parts sand to make an excellent cleaning solution for under your refrigerator." Or, "Be sure to scrape the wax off your kitchen floor on a day it's not raining." Or, "Old newspapers are excellent for cleaning ceilings made of porcelain." And this one: "Be sure to vacuum your family as they enter the house to prevent them from bringing in dust and dirt."

None of this helped much. Don't get me wrong. I would have liked a nice clean apartment, an uncluttered one with the empty look, the Japanese look: a mat for a bed, a kitchen consisting of just a cold water tap, a table without chairs and chairs without a table, a potted orchid in the corner and short poems written here and there on the walls. I would have liked that (who wouldn't?), but it would have taken me about six years to achieve that. Not bad, considering that I had been living there for two whole months.

Read these poems and this will happen to you, too.

The Agatha Poems

This chapter includes the world famous, never-before-published "Agatha Poems." Though many scholars think these poems were discovered by Eddie Cantor in an ancient Egyptian pyramid, I know better. I wrote them. Why? Well, I'll be honest. I want to be a poet. I want to write for snobby literary journals like the "Paper Pen Journal" or the "Ringworm Review." Although I've been writing poems for years (two), only lately have I started wearing a long black scarf and looking confused. Though many of my poems are still coming out completely understandable, I'm working on that. Today's poets insist that: 1. Poems never rhyme. 2. Poems never make sense. And so, without further ado, and without the slightest mention of Maya Angelou, here are the Agatha Poems.

Agatha's Trip

Agatha flew
on a
plane.

(She thought
the whole thing
rather insane.)

She even had
a window
seat

beside an
old man named
Hecter C. Pete.

She wished
the plane would
go much faster.

She spilled
her lunch.
It was a disaster!

She asked to
speak to the
pilot and all.

To ask for a
parachute for
her doll.

She hoped
the plane
would soon
land

in a lot
of nice soft
sand.

Agatha's Doll

Agatha's doll
was very pretty.
It was handmade
in a foreign city.

She called it
Miggy Miffin Magee,
and always served
it a cup of tea.

She said that
her doll could talk,
although it
couldn't even walk.

But what was most
strange of all
was the language
of this talking doll.

English she didn't
seem to know.
She spoke Chinese,
but very slow!

Agatha's Cake

Agatha wanted
to bake a cake,
not having the
necessary time
it takes.

So she filled
her mother's pan
with quantities
of pretty sand.

She put it in
the oven on high,
and it exploded
to the sky!

Agatha's mother
was all shook,
and sent Agatha
to learn to cook!

Agatha's Birthday

Agatha's cousin
Sally O'Dell
gave her the gift
of a small bell.

Agatha's cousin
Susie O'Reilly
gave her a book
of which she thought highly.

Agatha's cousin
Betty O'Toole
gave her some thread
wound on a spool.

Agatha's cousin
Dizzy O'Duck
gave her nothing
and wished her luck!

Agatha's cousin
Cindy O'Malley
gave her a hat
from an old alley.

Agatha's Book

Agatha read
only one book,
and it was about
Captain Cook.

She wanted to go
out and explore,
for she found her hometown
quite a bore.

She read it
once every day
and wished that she
could sail away.

To seek adventure
was one of her wishes,
but her mother said,
"Go do the dishes."

She wanted to go
to far off seas
and find the fish that
she read could sneeze.

Agatha's Poem

Agatha decided
to try poetry.
(I wish she hadn't,
between you and me.)

So here is
the poem she wrote.
She called it,
"Sidney the Goat":

"There once was
a goat named Sidney,
and he was as silly
as he could be.

"He chased a fox,
and ate a pear
and jumped over
a polar bear.

"He skipped through
the garden at home.
It's hard to rhyme
When writing a poem.

"Sidney was a
a wonderful goat.
This is the
last poem I'll ever wrote."

Agatha sent in
her poem for a prize.
She didn't win.
No surprise.

Agatha's Singing Day

Agatha sang
a song today.
She spent the day
singing away.

When Alice
wanted her
to play,
Agatha sang, "Go away!"

"Agatha! Agatha!
What did you say?
Agatha! Agatha!
Want to play?"

Agatha still
sang her song,
not thinking it rude
or even wrong.

So Alice screamed
the whole day long.
The lungs of both
must be strong!!!!

Agatha at School

Agatha
finally
went to
school.

Although
she thought
it very
cruel.

She told
the teacher
she was
wrong.

She led
the class
in singing
a song.

She wrote
her name
upon the
board.

She told
a joke.
(Everyone
roared!)

The teacher
called her
mother
to say,

"If you'll
keep her
home I'll
even pay.

Agatha's Brothers

Agatha's brother
Timmy Jimmy
always said,
"Gimme! Gimme!"

Agatha's brother
Johnny Jerry
was very prone
to worry.

Agatha's brother
Ricky Nicky
hardly ate,
for he was picky.

Agatha's brother
Willy Billy
always laughed.
He was so silly.

Agatha's brother
Bobby Robby
collected rubbish
as a hobby.

Agatha's brother
Holingsworth the Third
had a name
that was absurd.

Agatha's Cat

Agatha's cat.
She named
it Rat.

Agatha cat
slept on
a mat.

Agatha's cat
was
very fat.

Agatha's cat
only
sat.

Agatha's cat
ate
her hat.

Agatha's cat
was a
brat.

Agatha's cat
was just
like that.

Agatha's Taxi Ride

Agatha's first
ride in a cab
was rather dull
and also drab.

It was just like
riding in a car.
It didn't go fast
or very far.

When she arrived
back at home,
she tipped the driver
with a pretty stone.

Agatha's Hat

Agatha got
a brand new hat.
(The old one was
eaten by her cat.)

Her new hat
was red and green;
had flowers on top
and feathers in between.

It had a large,
orange bow
and purple
pansies in a row.

It had some fruit
on the side
and a brim that
was very wide.

It had many ribbons
of colors bright.
Yes, her hat was
quite a sight!

It would have looked
good on her hair
except it was
too heavy to wear!

Agatha's Garden

Agatha's garden
was very small.
It hardly was
a garden at all.

She watered it
four times a day
until it finally
sailed away!

In fact it only
had one plant
given to her
by Mrs. Grant.

Agatha's Friend

Agatha's Friend
Maggie Mulroon
lives on a street
called Kippedydoon.

Best of all,
they like to wear
their mothers' hats
and wigs of hair.

They like to play
hide-and-go-seek.
They played it twice
just last week.

Royal ladies
they are, you see,
as each commands,
"Pass the tea."

They like to read
story tales
of Chinese cats
and fishy whales.

Let's pump up our sense of humor.

How To Increase Your Sense of Humor

In this chapter, I'd like to consider how to increase one's sense of humor. (As you probably guessed from the title.) Now, you're probably asking yourself two questions at once. One is, why would a person want to have a better sense of humor? and the other is: can a sense of humor be increased, improved or extenuated? The answers are, True, False, True, True and None of the Above. Just kidding. To answer the second question first: Yes. Now, to answer the first question second: an increased sense of humor will make your life better.

Here's how. (Now, pay attention.) If you increase your sense of humor—make it more active, that is, bring it into play more often, you'll be happy (i.e., worry less, have fewer fears, be kinder and more patient). The idea is that a lack of sense of humor is a way to take life, situations and a clogged drain too seriously. It's also a way not to take hurts, unkindness, rudeness and living in New York City too seriously. Having a sense of humor will help with this. (Yes, I am repeating, but the publisher wanted the book longer.)

By increasing your sense of humor, you increase your happiness level, and I think (sometimes, I do think) that makes you more "open" to moving to an island off Greenland and accepting the natives' decision to make you their king. Now, you may be asking yourself another question, and if you're asking yourself, why do I have to answer it?!—that is, how? What do I mean, how? You really aren't paying attention to your own questions. How to increase your sense of humor? (That's better.) A sense of humor is a sense of, or a noticing of, things that are funny. To "see" the funny. A sense of humor is both a gift and a talent that can be developed. How?

— Be on the lookout for "the funny" in situations, conversations and in life in general.

— Comment on "the funny" when you notice it.

— Laugh at "the funny."

— Be ready to take life lightly. As someone said, "Don't take life too seriously; it's only a temporary situation."

— Be loving. Now that one might have surprised you. But being loving, compassionate and merciful will not only give you a brighter outlook on life, it will also give you a greater sense of humor. To wake up each day and start out in a loving way (after you've smashed your alarm clock) is really the best way to live. Now, it's easy to be loving to people who are loving back. But in difficult situations, or with people who are not loving, be loving anyway. The great Spanish mystic and poet, St. John of the Cross, said, "Where there is no love, put love, and you will draw out love." By your adding love to the situation, or giving love to the person, you will feel love, others will receive love, and—heck, there'll be love all over the place.

A sense of humor is something that grows and grows. It is something we should work on every day. First, have a sense of humor. Then be funny. Being funny (usually) flows from a sense of humor. Or at least it should. Make people laugh. As the old song said, "Make 'em laugh, make 'em laugh, make 'em laugh!" Make children laugh, lonely elderly people, strangers you meet (even strangers you don't meet). Life's too short to not go around bringing joy, cheerfulness and laughter into the lives of others.

Having a good sense of humor is something people think they have. But we should check. We should give some thought to whether:

— we have a sense of humor or not.
— if it's really alive, healthy and active.
— how we can increase it.
— and whether we left the coffeepot on.

Another way to increase your sense of humor—I have no idea what I'm going to write, but I have to make this chapter longer—oh yes, another way is to watch other people, those who have a really well-developed sense of humor. They may be professional comedians or just someone you work with. Watch them, watch people's laughter-reaction to them.

A sense of humor is truly indispensable to living calmly, sanely and happily in our world today. Mary McDonald wrote, "If you haven't got a sense of humor, you haven't got any sense at all." Yeah, life's hectic, frantic, etc., etc., but a sense of humor will help us get through the day, get through life and maybe get us through Friday afternoon. Hey, I have a question—if everybody is so stressed out, overworked and downright busy, who has time to watch the afternoon soaps? It's just a thought.

Another thing about having a good sense of humor is—well, that's it, I can't think of anything else to write. I have said everything I can think of about a sense of humor, and I can't find my book of Emerson quotes. Boy, did that guy write down a lot of neat quotes, or what? He'd be able to make this chapter longer. I just can't get my writing long enough. I wonder how Stephen King does it. Anyway, since we're here together and I have no idea what I'm writing about, let me just say that I'd like to take this opportunity to

— Thank you for buying this book (you're helping to feed the monks at this monastery).

— Ask you to write to me. (And I'll pretend it's fan mail and that your insults are an attempt to be funny.)

— Tell you that my birthday is September 21 and that I love to receive presents. If you're a millionaire or a billionaire (Hello, Mr. Trump) please send money.

— Tell you that I just can't think of anything else to write, not even any more stupid things—so this chapter's done.

"A joke is a very serious thing."
Winston Churchill

My gorilla's name is Fritz, of course.

What's in a Name?

If you really get into humor you may become so embarrassed you'll want to change your name.

I'm fascinated by the names of comedians. They are usually short. Sure, you can become famous as a singer named Engelbert Humperdink, but not as a comedian. Comics have names like:

> George Burns
> Toddie Fields
> Joan Rivers
> Bob Newhart
> Lily Tomlin
> Sid Caesar
> Fanny Brice
> Jay Leno
> Miss Piggy

These names are so short they make David Letterman seem like a sentence. But the thing that amazes me most about comedians is the use of Allen. It's an ordinary, simple, totally unfunny name. But just think of it. There's

> Gracie Allen
> Fred Allen
> Steve Allen
> Tim Allen
> Woody Allen
> Allen Klein

"What's in a name?" Shakespeare asked. "A rose by any other name would smell as sweet." I don't think so. What if it were called a Voosenmeyerwattleweed? We wouldn't even plant them. You'd think with an easy name like Craig, my life would be simple. It is if I just remember to respond to Greg, Gregg and Creep. Sometimes I get letters to Bother Cregged. My last name is Driscoll, but sometimes it gets written Driswell or Dresswell. Craig's not so bad considering the names of my three sisters—Clodamier, Anaxanora and Zoraeed. And they wonder why their singing act has never succeeded!

"For humor there must be a disciplined eye and a wild mind."
Dorothy Parker

So I'm now a medium. I used to be a large.

The Newest Age

I have no interest in New Age. To me, it's all a bunch of lies, stupidities and nonsense. (I'm always so tactful.) But all my friends (both of them) are interested in New Age things. Once, one of them talked me into going to a New Age meeting. I went only to refute all its stupidity. My friend Sidney took me to a seance. He got to the monastery just after supper. The evening went like this—

"Brother, where did you get that chair? I never saw it before."

"I got it this week. I bought it at the Salvation Army."

"You bought a used chair? Don't you know that old furniture can give off bad vibes? If the people who had that chair had an argument with the chair in the room; well, you're in big trouble."

"What if I bought a new chair and the people at the factory had an argument? What then?"

He didn't answer but kept his distance from the chair, so I said, "What are you worried about? You're wearing your magic crystal."

"It's not magic. It has power."

"So activate your power-enhanced crystal."

"I can't do that unless I go into a trance."

"I thought you were always in a trance."

No answer. So I said, "Do you want me to move the chair?"

"No! It will activate the bad vibes. Let's just go. Anyway, we'll be late for the seance."

"How can we be late? Won't the psychic know we'll be late and wait for us?"

"Brother, psychics don't know everything. They just know certain things."

I guess they just know what they are paid for. Anyway, we got to the psychic's house and a small group was sitting around a table. The psychic was at the head of the table and didn't look at all like a gypsy, as I had expected. There was a man who looked like Walter Matthau would look wearing a Shirley Temple T-shirt, a lady with a French poodle with blue-gray hair (the lady, not the dog), a couple of college students and a man in a U.P.S. uniform. The psychic began.

"Since this is Brother Craig's first seance we'll let him go first."

So I said, "I'm thinking of a state that begins with the letter U."

To which the psychic (her name was Slurp) said, "No, Brother, please pick a famous person you wish me to channel.

Her contempt for my ignorance was poorly hidden.

So I said, "Oliver Twist."

"Brother, I can't conjure up a fictitious person. A real person, please, from history."

"Okay, Harry Truman."

The psychic rolled back her eyes, ate a bagel and said, "I'm from Missouri. Show me. Ask me anything."

"Okay, give me a lottery number to win millions of dollars."

"I can't answer that."

"Great!" I said, thinking once again that psychics can

never make one a millionaire. "Okay," I said, "Mr. Truman, just give me some good advice."

"Never wear dirty socks."

"What! My Aunt Twaddle calls me every morning collect from Cleveland to tell me that. I don't even need an alarm clock."

"My time is passing. Call another spirit," said Mr. Truman.

Sidney said, "I call Cleopatra."

Then the psychic jolted or burped and said, "The Nile is a very boring river. I am Cleopatra."

So Sid asked, "What was Richard Burton like?"

"A nice man; gave me a big diamond."

I looked to make sure where the exit was.

"Call another spirit. My time is passing," said Cleopatra.

Boy, it was really moving fast, this psychic ought to switch to another long distance company.

The Walter Matthau-type guy asked for Einstein. (He must go to movies.)

"$E=mc^2$," said Einstein.

"Mr. Einstein, I'm so honored. Please tell me, I've been dying to know. How did you like living in Princeton?"

"A nice town."

"Mr. Einstein, what do you think of quantum physics."

"Never understood it. Goodbye."

At that point the psychic collapsed on the table. Then the table collapsed. When she recovered she served some fruit juice. When the table recovered it served the chips. Then the psychic collected $35 from each person. Sydney paid for me, after I insisted. Then we left. On the way home, Sidney and I talked.

"Wasn't it fascinating, Brother?"

"Like watching 'Bowling for Dollars.'"

"Didn't you enjoy it?"

"All their answers were nonsense."

"That's because you don't understand. The spirits were speaking in symbolic words. When Cleopatra said, 'The Nile is boring,' she meant we're all going to have a financial crisis."

"Yeah, thirty-five dollars' worth."

"And when Harry Truman said, 'I'm from Missouri; show me,' it means that grapefruit prices will go up."

"More bad news."

"And when Einstein said 'E=MC squared,' he means either that the Yankees will win the World Series, or we'll all die tonight."

"That's nice," I said, trying not to laugh.

"Oh, Brother, you don't understand. New Age is so great, it enlightens me so much. Before I got into it, no one considered me an intellectual."

"Is that so?" I muttered as he pulled into the monastery's driveway.

"Well, good night, Brother."

At home I kept thinking: those people are nuts and that was the stupidest evening I have ever spent since the time I went to see six Spencer Tracy movies in a row. I mean it was such a lousy evening. It must be all the fault of that chair.

*"The humorist, like the wild animal,
always walks alone."*
Søren Kierkegaard

I see that you will read the next chapter.
Well, maybe not.

More New Age Stuff

Let me tell you about my other New Age friend. I'll call him "Sam" because that's his name. He recently told me, "I know beyond a question of a doubt that I'm the reincarnation of Napoleon."

"How can you be Napoleon? You're not even short," I said.

"That doesn't matter. In my last life I was Napoleon. Before that I was James Beard, Julius Caesar and Truman Capote."

"How can you prove it?"

"I dialed a 900 number and the psychic told me so."

"Oh, so it's scientific?"

"Of course, the psychic even knew my phone number."

"Did she know her own? Anyway, what good does it do if you were all those dudes before?"

"Just think of all the information I have, I mean we have, in our collective memory."

"Enough to make lunch."

"I mean, I can speak with the wisdom of Caesar."

"So tell me how to make a salad."

"I can make brandy as well as Napoleon did."

"Yeah, and with James Beard and Truman Capote you can make flaming rice pudding, write a novel and talk funny."

"You don't understand, Brother. You are unenlightened because you grew up in New England."

"What does that mean?"

"New Englanders are predisposed to being unenlightened."

"Great, that's like saying I'm programmed to be de-programmed."

"Sort of. Besides, you don't believe in mind travel."

"What's that, like a courier?"

"No, it's when we let our minds wander to other places, other worlds and other times. You never did that?"

"I do each time I ride in a cab."

"Oh, Brother, get with it. New Age is the way to go."

"I don't want to go."

"Are you saying you are happy even though you're unenlightened, dull, not-with-it and old-fashioned?"

"No, I'm saying that I don't believe that a crystal will make me happy. A few diamonds, maybe."

"But you have to understand that the stars control our lives."

"So it's Hollywood, not Washington!"

"No, I mean astrology. What sign were you born under?"

"Boston Maternity Hospital."

"I mean your zodiac."

"I had it removed with my tonsils."

"You're hopeless. You simply are a unilevel person."

"A what?"

"You have no second self, no third eye, no alter spirit that controls you."

"Thank God."

And, you know, New Age is a big business. There are books, videos, conferences and time-travel cruises. People spend lots of money to call someone to ask who they should marry. Don't they have a phone book?

And the fortune tellers! They deal out a bunch of cards and tell you someone will enter your life who will rip you off (that's the fortune teller) that you will know joy and sorrow and that it will rain next Tuesday. They get their lead from the person who is asking the question. I saw it on TV. "Will I find a new boyfriend?" asked a woman. Madame Zeldini answered, "I see that your last relationship was not good." Questioner nods vigorously. "It was a real problem." Questioner smiles knowingly. "The guy was a creep." Questioner looks amazed at the psychic's power. Celebrity host smiles financially. I marvel at the psychic's ability to read the obvious in the questioner's expressions. "Your next boyfriend will be perfect. He'll look like Mel Gibson, be a Harvard graduate and a billionaire. You'll meet him tomorrow." Questioner beams, cries, jumps up and down, gives the psychic a big tip. "Isn't she marvelous?" the celebrity host asks. "Call now, our 900 number. All your problems will be solved at $3 a minute. We have genuine live (?) psychics waiting to help you. Call now. Visa and MasterCard accepted." It's all so stupid.

Then there was the ad I saw in the paper the other day: "You can be anyone you want to be. We can channel you into another time or you can be anyone from history. You choose. You can be Paul Revere, Sarah Bernhardt or Bette Davis (some fading may occur with time). Be the great person you've always dreamed of being. Why stay the loser you are now? Call us today, or write for our free book ($18.50 for shipping and handling): 'Channeling for Stupidos.'"

Or this one. A help wanted:

"Psychic needing assistant to do various odd jobs.
Forward my mail when I'm in the past or the future.
Feed my cat while I'm gone.
Make light lunches.
Apply in person to Wendy Wonderworker."

Of course, I'm always tactful and ever-so-subtle—so let me say: *New Age Is Old Lies!*

Yes, humor can help make us happy!

Humor and Happiness

More and more, research is telling us that for years we've had things backwards or at least sidewards or sideways. And our new understanding is all thanks to psychoneuro-immunology! Of course it is! What am I taking about? All right already, I'll tell you.

First, psychoneuroimmunology is the study of how our thoughts and emotions affect our health. We used to think that we smile because we are happy. Now we know that smiling can make us happy. We used to think that we thought depressing thoughts because we were depressed. Now we know it's those thoughts that cause the depression.

Much scientific and medical research is now teaching us that the egg comes before the chicken and we've been put-ting the cart before the chicken all "awrong." Then, again, we should have known all this because the book of Proverbs says, "As a man thinketh in his heart, so is he." Of course, that applies to women, too.

When we laugh, we send endorphins to our brain, where they have a party. And that makes us happy! But people wait around to experience something funny and don't get their daily requirement of humor, so they ain't so happy so they don't get so many endorphins up to their brain. I say, go out and look for humor! Look for things to laugh about if you really want to be happy.

Remember, happiness is not a given, it's an achievement. (Oh, how I wish someone would put that on a bumper sticker.) Immanuel Kant said, "God wants us to be happy, and he wants us to make ourselves happy." Moving right along, let me tell you that Dale Anderson, M.D. has some interesting things to tell us in his book *Act Now!* (Chronimed Publishing). We can even "fake" a smile, a happy expression and a laugh, and get plenty of endorphins for our money. "It has been shown that the endorphins can be 'faked' up. For instance, forcing a smile or a laugh can fool the endorphins into life. That's a great reason for laughing more, even if the situation isn't necessarily funny. Consciously being more optimistic, and looking for the humorous side of everyday events can give us that inner high." So fake it and laugh. I won't tell if you won't.

So the point: by having a sense of humor, by being funny and by laughing, we can help to make ourselves happy. And we are doing this in a direct way, through the way our mind and body operate. We might often think about how valuable humor can be in a difficult situation. But we should realize that it is also helpful in dull situations. Rather than giving in to a feeling of boredom, or what's-the-use-of-it-all, we should try to activate our sense of humor and try to do and say funny things—all this can lead us out of dullsville and into happiness.

Lately, I've been reading a lot of things that say that the act of praying or helping people helps us to be healthier. When we do these things with joy, good cheer and, yes, even humor, we help ourselves to be happier.

Although I believe that humor helps us to be happy, I think that encouraging people to believe that happiness is important is difficult these days. We live in a time that advocates and promotes doom, darkness, drama and dreary—I call it the Four D's Club. So many books, both fiction and nonfiction, so many films, songs, etc., are dark, sad—about suffering, violence and death.

Where are the happy books like *Please Don't Eat the Daisies,* by Jean Kerr? Where are the happy films like so many of the great musicals of yesteryears? Where are the happy songs like, "Singing in the Rain," and the one with the line, "I want to be happy, but I can't be happy 'til I make you happy, too," from, "No, No Nanette?" I make no apologies, I'm a happy person, and I like happiness, sunshine and that yellow "smile face"!

I think the most significant takeover by sadness in our society today is seen in clothing and fashions. Everything is dark-colored, usually black, baggy and depressing. Doesn't anyone wear yellow clothing anymore? Why can't we have comfortable, well-fitting clothes that are in bright, cheery colors?! I just can't believe it when I see young female singers who have finally gotten on a national TV show and they are wearing black pants and a black T-shirt! Why don't they wear a gorgeous peach-colored gown with yards of butterfly-wing-like cloth attaching the sleeves to the gown? Why don't they wear diamonds and beautiful jewels? Why don't they wash their hair? Then, again, they've chopped most of it off.

Everywhere I look, I see sad, dismal and dark. In more ways than one we need to lighten up, folks. Now, maybe you don't think that externals: say, clothes and grooming, affect a person, making him or her either happy or sad. Well, I think they do. They surely affect me! More and more, research is telling us that we are affected by the colors around us. As Dr. Anderson, mentioned above (remember him?), tells us, "There are colors that seem to elate us and others that seem to depress us." I believe bright colors make us happy, colors like yellow and orange. Please note that these are light colors. I think plenty of light, especially sunlight, makes us happy, too. God said let there be light! So light colors and lots of light makes us happy.

Add to all that a light attitude toward life, lightness regarding problems and situations, a lightheartedness and the lightness that comes from humor and laughter, and we'll be all "enlightened" and happy!

I call this my David Brenner look.

America's Favorite Kneel-down Comic Monk

Okay, you've been good, you've read the book this far—which is amazing, but are you going to buy it or just stand there in the bookstore reading it? So here's a little treat for you—my standup, I mean kneel-down, comedy routine. And because you've been so nice, let me tell you something—skip this chapter.

(Imagine applause; in fact, imagine the whole thing.) "Thank you. Thanks. Well, I'll begin by telling you about myself. "I got into comedy for the money. But I found it pays more than rodeo. I can't convince my Aunt Twaddle ... she still does rodeo.

"What can I do? Show Biz is in my blood. I come from a family of comics ... my uncle is a politician.

"Of course, one thing I don't like about Show Business is all the expenses. Money spent to impress people. I'm really not good at that. But I'm good at imagination. For example, the other night a film star asked me where I got my scarf. I told him, 'Oh, a little place off Fifth Avenue.'... I didn't tell him it was my brother's apartment.

"I'm a monk. I don't even know the correct names. Until recently, I thought Gucci's was a pizza place. ... I once said to a famous director, 'Hey, shall we go to Gucci's for supper?' ... I think that's the only reason I've never been in one of his films.

"And the name dropping! I try, but I'm not good at it. I find it hard to work the names in naturally. I end up saying things like 'When Her Majesty the Queen of Guava Guava called me the other night, although I was with several heads of state, I accepted her collect call.'

"The other thing I don't like is all those talk shows. I hate them. I hate it that they don't invite me.

"What amazes me is that so many performers are doing other things, like aerobic videos ... even Miss Piggy!

"I was really surprised the other day. One store had a 'Stretch and Slim' video by a whale.

"Lots of celebrities write books. Mostly autobiographies.

"Most of these books have catchy titles like 'My Life of Fame and Wealth' or 'I'm the Greatest.' And then, in small print, 'as told to.' What did they do, telephone an English teacher?

"Or, there are those biographies of stars that other people do. Half of them brag that they are authorized, the other half brag that they're unauthorized. The unauthorized ones are easy to write. You just cut out things from gossip columns and scan them into a computer.

"But why is everyone so interested in the stars? Big deal!

"Then again, nobody has written my life story ... people have written me off ... I don't even get fan mail ... except one letter from a lady in Idaho ... 'Dear Brother Craig, I'm writing to ask you a favor. Please, kindly send me a Mel Gibson autograph.

"I must accept my fate. I must go through life being a minor star. An opening act, with a little luck, for the biggies, the mega-stars like Selma Smith, the lady who spills plates-on-pols.

"But who cares? I'm doing what I like. I give hope to young comedians ... who have no talent. My words of wisdom to them are: anyone can be funny. The important thing is, when you look at yourself in the mirror each day ... you can honestly say ... you have hope; at least your not America's favorite kneel-down comic monk."

"No matter what your heartache may be,
laughing helps you forget it for a few seconds."
Red Skelton

Sometimes I surprise even myself.

The Power of Positive Laughter

Being funny is great. So is laughter. Laughter is a gift, given by God. Laughter is good, light, cheerful and joyous. G. K. Chesterton wrote, "Laughter is a leap." Laughter is the language of children. We need to laugh more. We need to help others laugh; little laughs and strong, hearty laughs. We need to give more laughter to the world, to help people cope and to relax, to be calm. We should meet tense situations laughingly.

I'll never forget the time I was held at gun point (well, sort of).

I was entering the building where I was staying (a student's residence) when I heard gunshots, and then a car pulled up, a man with a gun jumped out and asked if I had seen a white car. I was petrified, afraid and a little scared. "Did you see a white car?" he demanded. "White? I did see a car," I said, "but it was off-white, or a cream or rather a beige." He said, "Quiet, please." Rather polite for the setting. Then he asked, "Did you see any white car?" To which I answered, "Wait a minute, buddy! You may have the right to aim your gun at me, demand color-coordinated automobile data, but don't say 'any' white car, say a white car! I will not be spoken to ungrammatically!"

He said he was sorry. Then I said, "And, furthermore, you could hurt someone with that gun!" He put it away. Then I added briskly, "And, finally, I've been trying to sell some raffle tickets, and (getting tough) I think you better buy a few." He bought four. They were for an all-expense-paid trip for 280 people to Pago Pago. After that, he drove away. Then my friends came to my rescue. I was rushed to the police station to describe the person who had threatened me with a gun. My description ran as follows: "Tall, very tall, short, fat, quite skinny, young, old. He had a gun. He was driving a white car."

Laughter, we are told, is the best medicine. Oh well, I'd rather laugh until it hurts. Laughter is a very positive, upbeat thing. I really have great respect for Positive Thinking. I just want to borrow their title and change it a little: "The Power of Positive Laughter." What does it mean? I really don't know. Positive Laughter brings confidence. That sounds good. We all need confidence. Some of us need more confidence than we have now. Laughter brings Confidence. How to prove it? I think the best way to prove it (and to pass the buck to the reader) is to have you ask yourself the following questions:

— Can you feel unconfident while laughing?
— Can you lack confidence while making people laugh?
— Can you laugh while drinking water *and* driving a car?
— What was the middle name of the eighteenth president of the United States?

Anyway, laughing, and helping others to laugh, will make you feel more confident, more sure of yourself. Author Rita Mae Brown wrote, "Humor comes from self-confidence." Now, I suppose you know how helpful confidence is in helping you to be happy. But then again, maybe you don't, maybe you recently arrived from Tasmania or Jupiter, and you can't read English, and you weary from eating too many pickled cherries, so I'll explain the relationship of confidence and happiness in the simplest terms:

confidence = happiness.

Or, to be more precise

confidence = happiness.

Or, to put it in its philosophical terms

confidence = happiness.

Or, to put it simply: confidence × self-esteem + affirmation × retroactive self imaging = total awareness and self actualization × πr^2 × the hypotenuse of Freud's beard = the realization of the karma-induced nirvanahood state of consciousness-awareness and hypnotic being-ness with an accent on the zen-ness of total oneness and personhood with vital bean dip.

In other words, that's it in a nutshell. So laugh and be confident. Having a sense of humor and believing in the value of humor and being funny will help you be more confident. That's it.

I'll never forget the time (oh no, not again!) I was invited to speak to the "International Society of Jewelers, Watchmakers and Zoologists" in Dallas. My topic was "Yard Sales" and I did receive several standing ovations. (Isn't that what you call it when people stand up and walk out one-by-one?) After the talk I was invited to a reception, which I assumed was in my honor, at the home of a very wealthy juggler. There I was asked to answer several questions (unrelated to my talk) and to sing several songs at the piano. I was also asked to do the dishes. The point I'm trying to make is that I've completely forgotten the subject of this section. Oh, yes— confidence.

Laughter builds confidence. (I'll try again.) It's like this. Well, let's look at it from the negative side. Lots of people lack confidence. Many people lack self-esteem. You wouldn't believe how many people think they are losers. They really think that, and yet the truth is: everyone is a winner or could be. Why do people think little of themselves? Because they take certain aspects of their life too seriously—and precisely the aspects they don't like. If they are too short or too tall or too fat, then they let this affect their self-esteem. (Okay, if someone is too fat, he or she should lose weight for his or her health, but he or she shouldn't lack self-esteem in the meantime.) Or, people lack confidence because they can't do certain things, like play a certain sport, or learn a second language or fly without a plane.

Now, how does humor help people to build confidence?—I promise I won't drag this out. To put it simply, a sense of humor and a sense of what's funny, and a desire to be funny, all help us not to take ourselves, and those aspects of ourselves that we aren't too crazy about, too seriously. This really works! By gently laughing with ourselves and not belittling ourselves, we really can grow and grow in confidence.

"When humor goes, there goes civilization."
Erma Bombeck

Brother Craig pretends to read, while waiting
for Brother John to take the picture.

Waiting and Other Things

Patience is a virtue, but when I have to wait for anyone or anything, I find I need all the help I can get to wait patiently.

I hate to wait for anything. I hate waiting for buses, trains—I even hope to die quickly. My hatred for waiting is so extreme that I can't do crossword puzzles. I can't wait to finish.

Anyway, I can't just wait and not try. I do try to do *something* when I'm seemingly just waiting. I even bought a self-help book, *What To Do While Waiting*, at one of those fast book stores with a drivethru. But I didn't like its suggestions: 1. Read a book. 2. Knit. 3. Mentally clean your kitchen. None of that works for me. I prefer my own:

— Scream nonstop, and loudly.
— Smoke herbal cigarettes.
— Daydream in black and white.

— Practice parachuting.

— Ask strangers if they think I'm good looking.

— Count tires on passing cars.

— Write Dr. Pepper jingles in Japanese. (This really occupies me since I don't know a word of Japanese.)

— Sing arias from "Aida."

— Pretend to faint.

Usually, doing three or four of the above at the same time tends to help; that is, it gets my mind off the fact that I'm waiting.

All of us have things we find hard to do. It's got to be that way or self-help authors would be out of work. Of course, waiting isn't the only thing I hate to do. There are a few others.

— Waxing the TV set with petroleum jelly. (The fact that this serves no purpose and messes up the picture really gets to me.)

— Counting the number of times people say to me in a single day, "Do you think Hans Christian Andersen would like my hair like this?" I just hate that.

— Ironing cardboard boxes.

— Washing the dishes on Tuesdays, on Thursday, February 29th, and on the third Monday after the geese fly south.

— Being late for my origami class.

— Reading philosophy books while eating pitted raspberries while riding a bicycle. I hate that!

"All laughter is merely a compensatory
reflex to take the place of sneezing."
Robert Benchley

True, I do prefer Russian dressing
to Russian novels.

The World's Shortest Russian Novel

No doubt a few of my more unsophisticated readers are wondering why this book would include *The World's Shortest Russian Novel.* Well, for those of you who

— Do not believe a word I write.

— Have not read Igor Vinniszentacoff's book, "Why Brother Craig Put *The World's Shortest Russian Novel* in His Book *Humor Helps,* and Other Great Mysteries of Life Explained" (abridged, condensed and expanded edition).

— Think it's just for filler.

Allow me to say that it is just for filler. But here it is—

Chapter I

In the 1800's there lived in Russia a man named Ivan, a struggling playwright, who had written 4,872 plays. (None of which had been performed.) He was madly in love with the Tsar's daughter, Nicolaska. But he has been betrothed since childhood to Valiska, a ballet dancer with a Ph.D. in geophysics.

It was snowing. It had snowed for weeks, months, even days. There was snow everywhere. It was July. Ivan was walking down a busy street in St. Petersburg. He was thinking out a new play, planning how he would tell Valiska he didn't love her and wondering why the word "Thermos" is a registered trademark. Suddenly a man ran up to him, breathlessly, in a panic, and said, "Quickly, hurry; I have secret information for you. Please help me." Ivan said, "Come, we'll go into this tea shop." Settled in the shop, over a hot cup of Ovaltine, the man whispered his story.

"All my life I've waited for this moment. Now, I shall pass on my secret to you. I know I can trust you." Ivan sips his Ovaltine and wonders who will pay for it. The man continues, wiping his mustache with the tablecloth, Ivan's coat and the rug.

"My secret is so valuable you must tell me that, more or less, you won't tell it to many people, at least not today." Ivan said, "Sure," as he took off one of his boots and threw it into the fire.

"Here is my secret: I know how to get *Gentleman's Quarterly* for only $14.95 a year. And in Russian translation!"

Ivan wiped away a tear. His future would be secure now. All his dreams would come true. He decided to pay for the Ovaltine. At that moment the waitress came and set fire to the tablecloth (a Russian custom) and sang several arias from "Madame Butterfly" (a New Jersey custom).

Chapter II

Ivan waits outside the door at Valiska's house. To pass the time he invents the cellular phone. Finally, after six hours, the door opens. It is Nika, the maid, who speaks only Japanese. With hand signals, Ivan indicates that he is there to see Valiska, would like a sandwich, asks whether she knows any theater directors in Japan and if she has heard any good riddles lately. With a nod, Nika let him in.

Ivan waits in the drawing room and spends the time writing on the wall (which was okay because the wallpaper was pages from a crossword puzzle book). At last, Valiska arrives and says, "My darling, how good it is to see you. My love, my dearest one. Please, before you speak, let me ask just one question. What is your name, again?"

"My name is Ivan, and I don't love you. I'm in love with the Tsar's daughter, and I don't want to marry you. That's final. Is that okay?"

"Oh, Ivan. Oh, how could you? I have made all my wedding plans. I've rented the hall. Do you know someone else I could marry?"

"No," said Ivan, as he continued to do the crossword puzzle.

"Then, maybe I could have a Tupperware party. That's it. Oh, Ivan, do tell your sisters to come."

"I will. Then you're not angry?"

"Oh, Ivan, how could I be angry when the novelist who wrote this stupid story has decided otherwise."

"I see. Well, Valiska, I wish you much happiness. And, as a parting gift, I've brought you one-eighth of a chocolate bar."

"How can I ever thank you enough? A whole one-eighth!"

"Yes, but I've eaten out all the nuts."

"That doesn't matter. I shall treasure it always. I may even have it bronzed or write a poem about it or send it to the Smithsonian or perhaps to the Public Television Auction."

"Goodbye, Valiska."

"Goodbye, Nicholas. I mean, Ivan."

Chapter III

Ivan sits in his garret, writing a letter to Nicolaska. Here is the letter:

"To whom it may concern:

"I am madly in love with you. Please agree to marry me. I am a brilliant playwright, though not appreciated by theaters, actors or audiences. My plays are too avant-garde. The world isn't ready for them. They are all musical mimes.

"I am madly in love with you. Please marry me. If you don't agree to marry me, I'll: 1. Dedicate one of my plays to you. 2. See to it you are never mentioned in a Russian novel again. 3. Move to Florida.

"I am madly in love with you. Please marry me. I can assure you that if you marry me you'll be completely happy, as I know lots of really neat card tricks. Also, you'll be very wealthy (if you bring all your money with you). And you'll be unbelievably famous, as those great learned journals (some people call them tabloids) will proclaim throughout the grocery stores of the U.S.A.: "Russian Princess Marries Brilliant Playwright Whom Many Believe Is Elvis." Think of that. And also, I will promise to take you bowling every Tuesday night.

"I am madly in love with you. Please marry me. Who else could you marry, anyway? I am extremely handsome for a fat man. My face has two eyes, one nose, one mouth with two ears nearby. I like ice hockey, crocheting and sky diving. I speak several languages—don't smoke.

"I'm madly in love with you. Please marry me. I think you'd better, for several reasons: 1. If you don't, I'll write to you everyday. 2. I'll stop paying taxes (tell your father that one!). 3. I've talked the novelist who's writing this absurd story into this already.

"I remain, ever yours truly,
Ivan Dostuwekeycoagh, III, Esq., Jr."

Chapter IV

Amsterdam. Spring time. The annual tulip festival. The Vienna Philharmonic Orchestra is playing a Strauss waltz by Beethoven in C minor G with a circumflex Z. Boris, a waiter, Ivan's third cousin, is waiting on a table. When he stops waiting on the table and gets off of it—this speeds up the service.

"I'll have the watercress with mushrooms on rye and a diet Moxie," said Countess Wilma Von Haufenstauffe.

"Very good, Madame," said Boris.

Chapter V

Ivan is outside the Tsar's palace. He has waited for days to see Nicolaska or the Tsar or her mother or even one of the butlers. He has seen no one. He finally decides to take the paper bag off his head. Now, he can see a guard who says creatively, "What do you want?"

"I wish to marry the Tsar's daughter," said Ivan.

"Another one."

"Please lend me a uniform so I can sneak into the palace and at least speak to the Tsar about my fate."

"You've brought your fate with you?"

"No, should I?"

"Doesn't matter, I have an extra one."

"Please, what's your price?"

"Seven million rubles, two all-day passes to Epcot, fifteen Snickers bars, one sports card of Tiger Woods and an autographed photo of Betty White."

"Here, everything is in this package. Careful of the bow."

Ivan, disguised as a guard, works his way into the palace. After one week, he finds the Tsar's private study. Breaking down the door, very quietly, he enters, and finds the Tsar is working on his laptop computer.

"Mr. Tsar."

"Click on the mouse."

"What mouse?"

"Click on the mouse, press alt/C, then proceed to Windows."

"What windows?"

"Will you stop interrupting me? I'm trying to figure out my new program."

"If I help you, will you grant me anything I ask?"

"Of course."

"Will you let me marry Nicolaska?"

"Of course. What else?"

Chapter VI

Ivan and Nicolaska were married in April. Their reception was at George's Diner in Newark, N.J. At the reception, George read a poem. Here it is.

> There once was
> a guy named Ivan,
> who wrote plays
> while he was drivin.'
>
> He married a girl
> named Nicolaska.
> If you don't believe me,
> just ask her.
>
> Ivan's cousin—
> his name is Boris.
> He's a waiter,
> but once sang in the chorus.
>
> Valaska's not
> mentioned at all.
> By the way,
> my sister is tall.
>
> I now say
> without regret,
> This is the shortest
> Russian novel yet.

(Translated by Princess Melanie Borisnocope while drinking orange juice. All rights reserved. International copyright according to the Kiwanis convention at Berne. Reprinted with both necessary and unnecessary permission.)

Laughter is the best medicine.

To Your Health

Okay, so here we are at 74.9 percent through this book, more or less, so I thought you might need a break from laughing hysterically—well, maybe not. But anyway, this chapter is kind of serious. (Don't you just hate that word?)

Let's talk about how having a sense of humor, and laughing, helps our health. Well, we can't really talk about it unless you telephone me; but, anyway, get a cup of herbal tea and please keep reading. I think that when we are fit and healthy, we feel more like being kind, charitable, and taking better care of our prize-winning collection of live beavers. (You thought I forgot, didn't you?) When we feel full of vim and vigor we feel ready to get out there and make the world a better place. Or, maybe even find a better place to live than this world.

The question is: does humor and laughter help health? The answer, for $200 and a used car is—Yes!!! Now, to prove it.

Well, the book of Proverbs tells us, "A merry heart doeth good like a medicine: but a broken spirit drieth the bones." Now, I don't know about you, but I don't want dry bones! And Bernie Siegel, M.D. says, "Genuine humor is therapeutic." And John Cleece says, "Mental health is the ability to keep things in proportion. And what is a sense of humor but a sense of proportion?" But we're not talking here about mental health, so I wish John would stop interrupting and let William Shakespeare tell us: "Frame your mind to mirth and merriment, which bar a thousand harms and lengthen life." And Mark Twain said (in Tom Sawyer), "The old man laughed loud and joyously, shook up the details of his anatomy from head to foot and ended by saying that such a laugh was money in a man's pocket, because it cut down the doctor's bill like everything." And did your know that in 1928, Dr. James Walsh wrote a book called *Laughter and Health,* in which he noted that laughter often reduced the pain following surgery and seemed to promote the healing of wounds? But I can't find anyone else who has read his book.

You've got to hear about this! A physician in Sweden reported that six women who had painful muscle disorders found much relief during a thirteen-week program of humor therapy. During these weeks they read funny books, listened to funny tapes, watched funny videos and laughed themselves silly. They also made sure that they started giving humor a more important place in their lives—some of them put it right above the sink in their kitchen. Anyway, they also attended lectures on humor research. The patients who laughed the most showed the greatest pain reduction in the original muscle problems, but they were very sore from so much laughing.

The most famous example of how humor helps health is from the life of Norman Cousins, the famous *Saturday Review* editor (and a friend of Dr. Albert Schweitzer), who got relief from pain (from a collagen disease) by staying in a hotel room and watching funny films. Ten minutes of big laughs gave him two hours of pain-free sleep. He had his physician take repeated sedimentation readings. These showed that the laughing produced a five-point drop in the sedimentation rate, and it wasn't a one-time thing, but was cumulative.

Now, I have no idea what a sedimentation rate is, but I'm

impressed, and I presume that my readers are smarter and more *au courant* (that's not English) about these things. Anyway, all this laughter eventually cured Mr. Cousins! He went on to write *Anatomy of an Illness* (W. W. Norton) and *Head First—the Biology of Hope* (Dutton), and to be on the faculty at UCLA School of Medicine, where he established a "Humor Task Force" to support clinical research about laughter. Great guy! He once said, "Laughter serves as a cloaking agent. Like a bulletproof vest, it may help protect you against the ravages of negative emotions that can assault you in disease."

Of course, anyone, even I, can see that humor would be a great help regarding depression. Glenville Kleiser tells us, "Good humor is a tonic for mind and body. It is the best antidote for anxiety and depression." Here's a wonderful example.

A 95-year-old man was admitted to a hospital for depression. (That is, the *man* was depressed. It wasn't a hospital for depression or a depressed hospital—which I have experienced.) He hadn't eaten for days nor had he spoken. We're told the doctors were concerned. Well, I should hope so! A clown came to the hospital to visit the patients. He went into the man's room and, within thirty minutes, had him talking, laughing and eating, which is hard to do all at once, even if you are not ninety-five years old. The man lived for several more years. The clown stayed in contact with him. As far as I know, the clown is still alive.

The belief that humor helps our health isn't new. I've believed it for several days now. And Sid Caesar (wasn't he a Roman emperor?) said, "Laughter is a great release." Way back in 1260 to 1320 lived Henri de Mondeville who was a professor of surgery, and he said, according to someone who must have heard him and wrote it down, "Let the surgeon take care to regulate the whole regimen of the patient's life for joy and happiness and allow relatives and friends to cheer him; have someone tell him jokes." Good idea, Doc.

And 100 years or so ago, Thomas Addison, M.D. wrote, "Health and cheerfulness mutually beget each other. Laughter breaks the gloom which depresses the mind and dampens the spirit." And a few years ago, Bernie Siegel, M.D. said, "Show me a patient who is able to laugh and play, who enjoys living, and I'll show you someone who is going to live longer. Laughter makes the unbearable bearable, and a patient with a well-developed sense of humor has a better chance of recovery than a stolid individual who seldom laughs."

And while I'm quoting anyway, Mrs. Regina L. Kleekamp shares this: "I work extensively with senior citizen shut-ins. We have great hilarity and much laughter. Those with a joyful heart are so much more able to cope with their infirmities and bounce back after lapses of illness." And Dr. Joel Goodman, director of "The Humor Project," believes: "If people could laugh fifteen times a day, there would be fewer doctor bills."

Getting back to curing a case of "worries." (Okay, we're not getting back to anything.) Raymond A. Moody, Jr., M.D. has some good advice in his book *Laugh After Laugh: the Healing Power of Humor* (Headwater Press). He writes, "Laughter makes one expansive in outlook and very likely to give the feeling that the future need not be the subject of quite so much solicitude as is usually allowed for it." And the good doctor also tells us, "The effect of laughter upon the mind not only brings relaxation with it, so far as mental tension is concerned, but makes it also less prone to dreads [neat word, huh?] and less solicitous about the future. This favorable effect on the mind influences various effects on the body and makes it healthier than would otherwise be the case."

This physician also says, "Humor can make us better by enabling us to stand aside from things." And he tells us, "Over the years I have encountered a surprising number of instances in which, to all appearances, patients have laughed themselves back to health, or at least have used their sense of humor as a very positive and adaptive response to their illness."

And this just in. A recent study shows that laughter is healing according to a report in the *Journal of the National Cancer Institute*. In the first study, ten healthy men were shown an hour-long humorous video. Immediately afterward, their blood showed an increase in interferon-gamma, which is not a grandmother who interferes, but an important healing chemical in the immune system. As Josh Billings said, "There ain't much fun in medicine, but there's a heck of a lot of medicine in fun."

Continuing my medical research, which would do credit to Dr. Salk, Dr. Spock or even Spock, I found something in a book called *One Life to Laugh,* by Donna Enoch Nelsen, Ph.D. (Potentials) Here's the quote: Ready? "Laughter stimulates the immune system, thereby increasing the resistance to disease. The thymus, the head of the immune system, shrinks under stress. When we laugh, we exercise the thymus, causing it to work more effectively." So let's laugh and exercise that thymus!

I recently read an article about how our emotions greatly affect our health. I can't find the article now, so just trust me. It's like this: LE=S and HE=H. That translates to: Lousy Emotions=Sickness and Happy Emotions=Health. Got that? And here's something from that wise and witty comedian, game show host (before your time), song writer and author of over forty books—Mr. Steve Allen: "Even if laughter were nothing more than sheer silliness and fun, it would still be a precious boon. But we now know that it is far more than that; that it is, in fact, an essential element in emotional health."

And here's something from Robin Williams: "For me, comedy is a tool. It's therapeutic. I use it as a release. You first start with yourself, making fun of yourself, then the world is open to you." And Patch Adams believes, "People crave laughter as if it were an essential amino acid." And Herb True advises, "Laugh about the little things in daily life that irritate all of us, and watch irritations vanish. By sharing laughter, you can put trivial problems in their proper place and in proportion to the whole of life. You'll remind others that it helps to take some things lightly, and you'll lift their spirits."

According to my notes, someone said that laughter gets rid of the feeling of fatigue. Someone else said it burns calories!!! So instead of eating that "Double Trouble Chocolate

Ruble," have a helping of laughter! Also, "According to a thirty-five year study (which is a long time to just sit and study) of ninety-nine Harvard graduates, men who had a positive outlook on life had substantially fewer illnesses later in life than the men who tended to concentrate on the negative aspects of their life." Yes, I know that last quote didn't mention humor. (And I can't remember who wrote it or where I read it.) You go ahead and make the connection between a positive attitude and humor. I'm getting tired.

Here's something interesting: Vera Robinson, Ph.D. is a nurse and professor emeritus of California State University Fullerton, School of Nursing. Bet you didn't know that. Anyway, Dr. Robinson's dissertation was on the importance of humor for health professionals. She's the author of *Humor and The Health Professions* (Slack Publishers). So take care of your health; pick a funny doctor. Of course, my doctor is funny—he's Jewish and from New York City!

In *Don't Get Mad, Get Funny*! (Whole Person Associates), by Leigh Anne Jasheway (great book; run out and buy it), we read about the benefits of laughter, which:

— Increases the antibodies in saliva that combat upper respiratory infections.

— Decreases serum cholesterol, thus providing an antidote for the harmful effects of stress.

— Secretes an enzyme that protects the stomach from forming ulcers.

— Conditions the abdominal muscles.

— Relaxes muscles throughout the body.

— Aids in reducing symptoms of neuralgia and rheumatism.

— Changes perspective.

— Makes you feel good.

— Has positive benefits for mental function.

— Improves ventilation, thus helping reduce chronic respiratory conditions.

— Reduces blood pressure and heart rate.

— Liberates interleukin-2 and other immune-boosters.

— Helps the body fight infection.

— Releases endorphins, which provide natural pain relief.
— Helps move nutrients and oxygen to body tissues.

Psychiatrist William Fry has studied humor for over thirty years. He is professor emeritus at Stanford University, School of Medicine. He also directs the Gelotology Institute. Gelotology is the study of laughter (seriously). Dr. Fry tells us that laughter activates muscles, increases heart rate and amplifies respiration. After a person laughs, he is relaxed and tension has been diminished. And listen to this: "A direct correlation between intensity of mirth and levels of catecholamines (hormones which cause the release of endorphins, the body's natural painkillers) was found."

Dr. Fry teaches, "Laughter is internal jogging. We have a lot of evidence showing that mirth and laughter affects most of the major physical systems of the body in a positive way. You can laugh a lot more times a day that you can do pushups."

Have I mentioned the immune system? The most convincing studies are those regarding immunoglobulin A, as no doubt you were just about to say. These little guys help protect us from respiratory problems like colds, flu and living in Los Angeles. This section of the immune system is sensitive to our moods. So when we are upbeat, happy, positive and enthusiastic, we'll fight off sickness quickly and then go on to something else. But when we are sad, depressed and spend the morning watching Jenny Jones, Maury Povich, Jerry Springer, Sally Jessica Raphael, Geraldo Rivera, Leeza, Ricki Lake and Rolanda, then we're in trouble.

Lee Beck and Stanley Tan have done studies showing that laughter strengthens the immune system. Two groups were established. One group watched a funny video. The other didn't. Blood samples were taken before, during after watching the funny video—and before, during and after not watching the funny video. Serum soritsol increases during stress because the brain sends a fax to the adrenal gland telling that dude to produce corticosteroids, which increase blood sugar and decrease the immune response. Dumb brain.

This team of researchers also learned that laughter increased activity in natural killer cells in the person laughing. These cells release a substance that destroys tumor cells and deadly viruses. Among people who have cancer, reduced killer cell activity is related to the spread of cancer.

Humor does help us to be healthy. But sickness is painful. Can we be humorous while we're in pain? We can and we must. Well, we must if we want to help ourselves be strong or brave during times of pain. The Danish philosopher Søren Kierkegaard wrote, "The more one suffers, the more, I believe, one has a sense of the comic. It is only by the deepest suffering that one acquires authority in the art of the comic." Or, to put it my way—suffering helps us be funny, and laugh (see Kierkegaard quote again), and laughter surely helps us when we're suffering.

"I personally believe that each of us was put here
    for a purpose—to build not to destroy. If I can
    make people smile, then I have served my purpose for God."
                                            Red Skelton

I finally made it! I'm a star!

About Tabloids

Totally unrelated to anything, here are my thoughts on tabloids. Those tabloids in the grocery store are really bizarre. The things they expect us to believe. Here are some of their titles, as I remember them:

— "The World Ended Last Tuesday." The paper came out on Thursday.

— "Giant Lizard Ate New York. Then Returned Home to Jersey."

— "90-Pound Woman Loses 120 Pounds."

— "Elvis Is Still Alive! He's in a Hospital in Memphis and He's Dying."

— "Aliens from Outer Space Landed in America. Disgusted, They Left Quickly."

— "Miracle Drug Stops Hair Loss. Only Side Effect Is Death."

— "Make 100 Million Dollars a Week—Printing Money."

— "You Don't Have to Pay Taxes. Just Go to Jail."

— "Martians Control Telephone Company."

— "New Weight Loss Diet! Lose Hundreds of Pounds Eating Only Stewed Paper."

— "Miss Piggy's Marriage to Kermit. Exclusive Photos of the Wedding."

— "Big Scoop! All Other Tabloids Tell Lies!"

It's ridiculous. How can people believe these things? It's almost as bad as believing the evening news. Why do people spend money on such publications? Or on books like this one?

"Humor is a sense of proportion
and a power of seeing yourself from the outside."
Zero Mostel

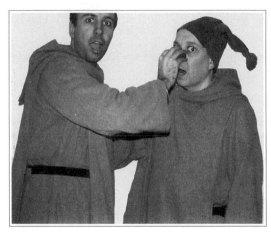

Brother John caught adjusting my clown nose.
Now that's humiliating!

Humble Humor

Humble Humor makes sense. It makes a great deal of sense to have a sense of humor and to laugh one's way through difficult situations. As Max Eastman said, "Humor is the instinct for taking pain playfully."

Like the time I spoke in Fritzwernd, Idaho. The convention center really was too large. There were only eight people in the audience. I was asked to speak by the Society for the Prevention of Boredom. My topic was "The Relationship Between Early Greek Philosophy and Place Mats," one of my favorite subjects.

The host introduced me lavishly by simply repeating the qualifications and background of the guest speaker who had to cancel, explaining that I had an M.D., a Ph.D., and an A.B.C. from Harvard in astrophysics, and incorrectly added that I would speak on "Wildflowers of Northern Greenland."

After such an introduction, I thought I'd better start with a joke—which nobody understood. Then, having cleared my throat for the eighth time, I was about to begin again when I heard a man say loudly and disappointedly, "I thought there was going to be a film."

Humiliating? No. Really funny? Definitely. As Walter Kerr said so wisely, "Laughter erupts precisely as the situation becomes hopeless." We have to look at (and love) ourselves with a sense of humor. It helps us to be happily humble if we laugh *with* ourselves.

Humor also is a great tension-breaker. I have a friend who is a master at this. When she is simply filled with (and surrounded by) tension, she does the funniest thing she can think of and, wham! there goes the tension—and sometimes the dishes. One evening, her husband's boss and his wife arrived for dinner. She discovered that she hadn't cooked the meal; that is, although the food was in the oven, she hadn't turned the oven on. She weakly thought of suggesting something like, "For fun we're having an M&M fondue party." Her guest would ask, "What is that?"—being totally uncultured and unfamiliar with the latest in nouvelle cuisine. "Why, that's when you fondue M&M's in chocolate pudding." But since she couldn't figure out how to skewer M&M's, she announced that dinner would be delayed about twenty-four hours and that sleeping bags would be provided. Before the guests (and her husband) could recover from that, she went into the kitchen and called nineteen of her friends, begged them to rush right over, not telling them why, and then went out the back door and spent the evening at the public library. Now, that's a sensible, humorous way to react to tension.

Humor is truly needed when you least expect it. Life, at times, needs comic relief. Be the one to turn a tense situation into a laugh situation rather than an argument. Relieve tension at meetings or at the dinner table by replacing negative vibes with humor. It works wonders. As Buddy Hackett said, "Comedy is a distraction, not an action. Humor takes your mind off the negative and turns it into laughter that's positive." Or, as Mark Twain said, "The human race has only one really effective weapon and that is laughter."

I recall once, when I was on a national TV talk show discussing "The Economy of China, Argentina and Boca Raton." An argument started between one of the guests (not me!) and a member of the audience over the relationship of these economies. Anyway, I could see that tension was building and the host had already taken eighteen station breaks (it was only a half-hour show), so I decided to interrupt. "Excuse me, but I think the answer really could best be explained by looking at the question from a philosophical or perhaps an anthropological, point of view; and, furthermore, before anyone interrupts me, I am going to do a tap dance for the rest of the two and a half minutes left in the show." Yes, humor works wonders. Try it—when others (and you) least expect it.

But the question could be asked—is humor habit forming or is it true that Napoleon hated truffles? To answer this question I will need to delve into Greek philosophy, Heidegger and a jacuzzi. This, of course, is going to be the most scholarly (and repetitious) part of this book, based as it is on a paper I read at the International Symposium for Nonsense at Geneva. (That's in Switzerland.)

I think I can explain this best—though I haven't any idea what I'm trying to explain—by telling about the time I applied for a job as a radio announcer at a small-town station, WZZZ. I had, at the time, no qualifications for that or anything else. Since then, I've learned cake decorating, lawn mower repair and how to make instant water. Anyway, I got the job, but the interview went like this:

Boss: Have you ever been on the radio?
Me: No.
Boss: Any experience or talent for announcing?
Me: No.
Boss: Any ability in running mechanical equipment?
Me: No.
Boss: You're hired.
Me: Could you tell me why?
Boss: No.

My first day began about twenty minutes later. I was on the air, and this is what I said for about half an hour (until I was fired): "Good evening (it was morning), ladies and gentlemen. I'm me, your announcer. I'm on the radio and you're listening to your radio somewhere, wherever you are. I'm here at the radio station, whose name I've forgotten, but you must know it because you've tuned in and I haven't. Now, for our first song, I'll play a record if I can find one. Here's one. I'll play it loud so you can hear it. Benny Bongington and the Electricians sing 'California, Here I Come.'" After playing the record, I decided to fill in for a while with commercials; but since I didn't have any, I just made them up and tried to keep them general, like "Go shopping. Shop at your favorite store and its favorite competitor. Buy things. Lots of them. Buy a car. Buy anything. Now, our next song is 'Bye, Bye, Blackbird,' sung by me because I can't find another record."

After this, I asked the listeners to call in, did more commercials and recited Egyptian poetry in hieroglyphics. I was just going to start offering prizes when the Boss came in and said I was fired.

Me: Will you tell me why?
Boss: No.

"*Humor is the foundation of reconciliation.*"
St. Francis de Sales

Looks like I'm the "Mercenary Monk."

Rich Reading

When I was a kid I wanted to be rich. When people asked me what I wanted to be if I grew up, I always answered the same—"A Kennedy." Now of course, being older and wiser, I no longer want to be rich. I just want lots of money.

Someone gave me a couple of copies of a magazine published for the super rich. I mean money. The magazine is unusual. First, it cost $10. I didn't pay much attention to articles such as "Men's Dress Shoes" and "The Top Twenty-one Caribbean Resorts." I mean, as a monk, I wear sandals, and I'll never live long enough to need twenty-one resorts in the Caribbean—twenty maybe but not twenty-one.

It was the ads that fascinated me—many for watches and even more for cars, real classy stuff. Also one ad was for pool cues (I wrote down the phone number). I now have all the information I need on where to get diamonds, handmade cigar boxes and expensive fountain pens. Considering I'm writing this on scrap paper with a souvenir ballpoint pen from Sid Jones Coffee Shop, the chances that I'll need any of these things are slim. Some of the pens have diamonds on them, which is very handy if suddenly you want to propose and don't have a ring. You hand the girl the pen—after having bent it into ring form, of course. Surely a unique, romantic touch.

There were ads for custom-made waterfalls, safari jeeps ($73,985) and a chance to herd cattle at a ranch where you pay for the honor!?! (I'm serious.) Then there were a couple of ads for companies that will search for and acquire anything you want. I want to be King of Greenland! I must remember to call them.

What was most interesting, because its practicality couldn't be argued, was a model train made of 14-carat gold (engine has 190 diamonds) and four gold wagons that are filled with rubies, emeralds, sapphires and diamonds. Only ten in the world. Originally sold for $100,000; sacrifice price, now $55,000.

But it's the Real Estate I need to check out. I can't decide—there's a ranch for $15,000,000, a house in Jamaica that rents for $10,000 a week, and 230 acres in Hawaii for only $1,200,000—and they're near an active volcano!!! Then there is a house in Illinois for $7,000,000, a hotel in the Dominican Republic for $3,000,000 and a villa in France for $8,000,000, that has a seven-car garage (but if I buy the house I'll never have enough money left over for seven cars; in fact, I'd have to ride the metro). Or I could rent a yacht with a helicopter—though why anyone would want to leave the yacht for a helicopter ride is beyond me.

And, seriously, do you know anyone who would like an attache case for $3,500? Hey, I could become an Honorary Consul for only $1,495 ,which might be a good deal except I really don't know what an Honorary Consul is. An etiquette course is also offered. It includes Power Eating. I know a teenage boy who does that and it's not a pretty sight.

Mind you, I mustn't forget the ads for cigar accoutrements, Bentleys, $150,000 stereos, custom carpets, antique dueling pistols (I'm not making that up), a letter signed by JFK (for $6,500—and not signed too neatly at that), Bengal cats that look like leopards, a 1950 soda fountain for a $1,000,000, a hotel and casino in Santa Domingo for $6,400,000 (I called, but the line was busy so they can forget it) and one for a private island dealer in case anyone needs an island.

My favorite ad was the one for the lie detector phone! That's right, if someone is talking to you on the phone and that someone lies to you, the phone indicates it. No, I don't know how. I don't think a voice hollers, "Hey, dummy, you've just been lied to. Are you going to take that?!" Probably a light goes on. Maybe the phone hangs up automatically. I don't know.

But how can a machine tell if someone is lying over the phone? Maybe if the person sounds nervous? Great, so it'll call all your nervous friends liars! Can a machine on your phone tell if the caller's hand is shaking? Oh wait, maybe the machine just listens to the caller's statement and decides if it is a lie. Someone says, "Yes, Louise, I lost fourteen pounds this week." And a machine hollers out, "No way, tubs! Who are you trying to kid?" Or, someone says, "Myself, I wouldn't want to be rich." And the machine says, "Right, you buy six lottery tickets a week—and you don't want to be rich!" Personally, I'd find a machine very distracting. Maybe that's because when people talk to me on the phone I'm listening, but I'm usually doing something else also, like doing the dishes, sweeping the kitchen or reading.

Ah, to be rich. Think of the things I could buy—just from two issues of a magazine. Of course, there were ads for guard dogs—no lousy burglar is gonna steal my gold train. No sir, better he be ripped apart. Ah, to be rich and gracious. And I didn't see any ads for books. Don't rich people read? Maybe they just read extravagant ads.

Do halos come a size larger?

Saintly Silliness

As a Catholic monk, I like to name-drop, using the saints. Actually, many saints were big on humor. As the poet William Cowper wrote, "True piety is cheerful as the day." And even better, G. K. Chesterton believed, "A characteristic of the great saints is their power of levity." As a monk, I have spent much time reading the lives of the saints. The saints have illustrated that holiness is cheerful. Many of the saints were not only cheerful—they were humorous. They were funny. And they had lots of fun.

That surprises us. Though we don't think of laughter as wrong, we're still surprised at saints giving time to such things. Yet they did. They realized that making others laugh, and encouraging themselves with laughter ,was a noble work. Following St. Paul's advice, the saints knew that "God loves a *cheerful* giver."

Often we don't know of the humor of the saints because the saint's biographer has left out the funny stuff. Years ago, in an article in *Vogue* magazine, poet and writer Phyllis McGinley complained that pious writers have made saints "all soul and no body. The pose them in plaster attitudes, hands forever uplifted, eyes cast down. They forget that what a reader wants is not a picture, but a motion picture. The stir of life is missing and so is ... the ripple of laughter. Most of all, I miss the laughter."

Yet many saints had a great sense of humor. Many were downright funny. St. Teresa of Avila was known for her sense of humor, her wit, and for bringing laughter and joy to the recreational times she and her fellow Carmelite nuns spent together. She would dance about the room and play the tambourine (she was a Spanish saint). When she was once publicly ridiculed and criticized, she tells us, she just enjoyed a "quiet laugh." When disappointed, she said lightly, "I don't know whether to laugh or weep." Her good friend, the Franciscan, St. Peter of Alcantara, stated that "with all her sanctity she always appeared cheerful and agreeable." St. Teresa even prayed, "From silly devotions and from sour-faced holy people, good Lord, deliver us."

St. Francis de Sales, the gentle bishop of Geneva, was known for his sense of humor. He's the one who said, "A saint who is sad is a sad saint." His religion classes for children were punctuated by much laughter, since the bishop illustrated his teachings with funny stories.

St. Philip Neri, a loveable priest who lived in Rome, is considered the funniest of all the saints. He would have half his beard cut off and walk around Rome like that, getting lots of laughs. He also would have his hair cut right outside his church; stopping people going in to ask if he was getting a good cut. When at the Vatican, he would pull (or tweak, to use the British verb) the beards of the Swiss Guards. Perhaps that's why they no longer have beards! To a worried priest, he said, "Come now, Father, let's run a race." And they did so, hand in hand. (Which seems to me to make winning the race kind of hard.) It is said that cheerfulness flowed from St. Philip. It is true that he often did funny things so that people wouldn't think he was a saint. But still, he must have been fun to be around.

St. Phillip's two favorite books were the New Testament

and a joke book. He once told a group that came to his house, "I will have no sadness in my house." He often walked around Rome in ridiculously large, white shoes carrying a bouquet of hay (and sniffing at it), laughing and singing, followed by friends and his fat, white dog. (I guess he got the dog to match the shoes.) Children loved him. Everyone loved him. Everywhere he went, people laughed.

St. Thomas More is known for his cheerfulness and humor, jesting even just before his execution. He paid the executioner, whom he said should be paid for his work. Then, just before he was beheaded, he moved his beard aside, remarking, "The beard hasn't committed treason." (Treason was the crime of which he had been falsely accused.)

St. John Bosco, or Don Bosco as he is better known, was a lighthearted saint. This surely must have helped him in his great work with troubled boys. He often told the boys jokes and funny stories. St. Therese of Lisieux, the beloved French Carmelite nun, is not well known for her sense of humor. Yet, during recreation in her Carmelite convent, she would do funny impersonations for the other nuns. St. Maximilian Kolbe, who was so devoted to the Virgin Mary, and a martyr at Auschwitz, would laugh so much at recreation with his fellow Franciscans that tears would roll down his face.

One story that really impresses me is about St. Caedmon. He was a monk in England ,way back during the days of the Anglo-Saxons. He was a good friend of the abbess St. Hilda of Whitby. He was also the first poet to write poetry in English; that is, Old English or Anglo-Saxon. The story that I find so inspiring is that, as St. Caedmon was dying, he jested with his brother monks who were with him. Now that's having a lasting sense of humor!

"I commend mirth." Ecclesiastes 8:15

Life can be tough. Wear a hard hat,
but keep smiling.

That's Life!

Here are several (more or less) columns, entitled "That's Life," that I am hoping will be accepted for national syndication, leading to a Pulitzer Prize, and maybe even payment. They were written in an effort to help people take life less seriously, to foster a lighter attitude and to bring joy, happiness and ozone into the lives of people everywhere. For as Seneca wrote a really long time ago, "It is far better to laugh at life than to lament over it."

Allow me to repeat. I believe that taking life less seriously, having a "lighter" attitude helps people to be happy. Studies at the University of Pomade (P.O. 010) have proven this to be true—at least with a group of ten or more on Tuesdays when it's raining. Anyway, here's the first column.

That's Life!

Some years before I became a monk, I became a health food freak. I went straight from junk food to granola nuts. I burned all my copies of *Sugar Monthly* and put up a poster of

Euell Gibbons. I instantly felt light and free and enjoyed the wind blowing through my hair—until I turned off the fan. I started reading books about bean sprouts and uncooked water. My whole life changed. I threw away my eyeglasses, preferring natural eyesight—until I tripped over an organic balloon (left over from a party I gave for the Society of Brown Rice Growers).

I really got into it. I even threw out the entire contents of my refrigerator: eighty-four boxes of snack cakes. I even had my cola service canceled. (I used to have it piped in to my kitchen sink.) Ever since I got into health food I can't stand going into a regular grocery store. One time, there I was in line with my whole wheat bread and tofu. Then I noticed what was in the carts nearby. One lady had a package of fatback, bacon, purple gelatin and sugar. The cart behind me was worse. The guy had whiskey, cigarettes and a book on exercise.

One day I thought I'd go nuts if I didn't speak out. An elderly woman (I mean, "youth impaired") had the following: nine pounds of butter, fourteen packages of cookies, marshmallows and Zimple Extra-Salty Soup. She weighed about 400 pounds. I felt I just had to warn her of how harmful these products are. So I reviewed in my mind the best way to say it diplomatically. Perhaps, "Hey, stupid, are you trying to get sick?" No, not that. Maybe, "I've seen better food in a pig sty." As I was still mulling this over, she spoke to me. "Excuse me, sir, but could you please reach over and hand me twelve things of Tic-Tacs, four packages of bubble gum, a set of false fingernails, two flash lights, four packages of corn chips and a *TV Guide*?" After doing all that, I began weakly, by saying, "I notice your culinary selections were not determined by the latest nutritional research or by wanting to live." She surprised me by smiling pleasantly, nodding her blue-gray wig and saying, "Now, sir, I know just what you mean. Don't worry. This food isn't for me. It's for my mother." Oh well, that's life!

That's life!

I'm really depressed today. I got another rejection from a publisher. That's my fifth one today. It was a play I really had my heart set on seeing performed on Broadway. Maybe even in a theater. It was a modern version of a Greek tragedy. I thought for sure that it would make it. I did my research really well. I read "Greek Tragedies from Sophistry to Hippicralies." That was my nephew's term paper. He's a sophomore in high school. He's twenty-seven years old.

My play's called "Dimitri's Diner." The first scene takes place in the diner. Though it's in a modern setting, it is designed for theater-in-the-round. The characters are: Demitri, head waiter; Gladys, his wife; their three sons, all named "Dimitri" (their sweaters are numbered); Nick, a cab driver with a British-Norwegian accent; a chorus of 2,000 people (off stage) and fourteen dancing snails (optional). Now, it's not the rejection I mind so much. It's the loss of the payment. You should see the letter I got back:

Dear Brother Craig:

Though we normally send a form letter explaining our nonacceptance of manuscripts, we have decided that this letter would not be suitable in your case. Our form letter explains that our nonacceptance does not reflect the quality of the manuscript submitted. In your case it does. Our editorial board felt that:

— Your manuscript was rotten.
— You're a lousy writer.
— The play was stupid.
— No one ever in the history of the world has ever written (or could write) anything so bad.
— You used one comma unnecessarily.

With every best wish I remain,

Bernard Babbington
Editor, Perfect Plays, Inc.

Of course, I'm not discouraged. I've decided to turn it into a musical comedy. I'm hoping Mickey Rooney will play Dimitri with Ruth Buzzi as Gladys and Robert Redford as the Cabbie. For songs, I'm just going to work in a lot of Benny Goodman stuff. The other four rejections I received all dealt with my three-volume scholarly study of the use of window metaphors in Haiku poetry.

Because of all these rejections, I went out and took a writing course. It was at the College of Creative Nothingness. Our small group met on Tuesday evening. It was taught by a woman named Margot Khklzqlph, who once had a short poem published in a small literary journal in northern Finland. She smoked unlit cigarettes. She taught the emote method. We sat around the room and followed her instructions.

"Now, my dear unpublished hacks, I want you to emote, to feel like what you are writing about. This time, emote a story about a cat." We meowed for twenty minutes. "Now, emote a Shakespearean sonnet, a cola jingle and a novel about Germany in quick succession." Some students got sick and had to leave the room. "Now, I want you to feel like a pen or a word processor. This will lend to greater understanding in your writing." I had a problem with this. I spent ten minutes trying to decide between a fountain pen or a crayon, which is what I usually write with. It was a stupid course; I dropped it after two years. Oh well, that's life!

That's Life!

Recently I was interviewed. That is, I got a call like this: "Hello, is this Brother Craig, the monk and writer?" When I admitted it, the guy said, "You, see, Brother, you have been chosen for a celebrity interview." To which I said, "What celebrity will interview me?" He laughed and said, "No, Brother, you're the celebrity. You are Brother Craig, the monk and writer?" I said, "Yes," and asked what publication was it for, naming some of the national ones. "Oh no, Brother, you see

it's for my term paper. I'm a freshman at Crumper Community College, and we have to write a term paper—it's due
tomorrow—on a celebrity, and you're, like, the only one in
town except that farmer who yodels. Anyway, he's busy. So
could I come over in twenty minutes and interview you?"

Wanting to do my part for educational causes, and grasp-
ing at any free publicity, I agreed. "Oh, thank you, Brother.
Please have your tape recorder ready."

He arrived four and a half hours later. A nice kid, weighed
about eighty pounds, his red hair waxed into points and three
rings in his left nostril. He parked his bike inside the monastery (chained it to the hat rack). We went into our living
room. We sat down. Then we got up off the floor and sat on
some chairs. He began with some nervous laughter that made
the rings in his nose jiggle. Both his ears were tattooed.

Kid: "Now, Brother Craig, what was the first thing you
ever wrote? You can answer 'yes' or 'no,' if you prefer."

Me: "The first thing was, I think, my name."

Kid: "Thank you. Do you consider yourself more a surre-
alistic novelist than a Heideggerian social critic?"

Me: "Yes."

Kid: "Among your works, say, those not listed as a Best
Seller or perhaps those you think should be, which do you
think is the least awful?"

Me: "My Handbook to Pebble Polishing."

Kid: "Of course. Now, there is talk of your recent nomination for a Nobel Prize in literature. Do you think that the fact
that you nominated yourself makes your chances slim?"

Me: "No."

Kid: "Thank you. Among the writers that influenced you,
how would you explain the encouragement you received from
Benjamin Disraeli, Dickens, Tolstoy and Peg Bracken?"

Me: "Yes."

Kid: "Thanks. Now, we haven't even touched on the subject of alcohol, drugs and altered states."

Me: "No, we haven't."

Kid: "Thank you. As a writer, how do you feel you make a contribution to society?"

Me: "By praying."

Kid: "My final two questions. Do you write for art, literary excellence, personal fulfillment or for the money, you hack, and could I have a cup of coffee?"

Me: "Three out of five, and do you take sugar?"

The next week I received a phone call. I had hardly said, "Duffy's Tavern," when I heard, "Oh, Brother. Oh! You won't believe it. The term paper! The interview! I got a C+. The highest grade I have ever received. My teacher was so ecstatic. She said I was a born writer with a very vaporous style, another A. A. Milne, a writer of genius, and that she had never heard of you." Oh well, that's life!

That's Life!

"I don't understand it," I said to the mechanic. "Again, you have to change a spark plug? You did it in 1973." He just sighed. As I drove back to the monastery, I thought about asking my superior if we could get a new car. But one does get so attached to a Gremlin.

Actually, when it comes to machines, I'm hopeless. I give off bad vibes or something. And the word is getting around. Just the other day, the lady at a public library said, "Brother, our director has decided that you can't use our photocopy machine again. You broke it the last time. The machine is not made to copy the things you did. First of all, you tried to copy the entire *Encyclopedia Americana*, then a wet oil painting and the screen of your laptop computer. And, Brother, you used all Canadian coins." I was offended, and told her that I'd never do a book signing at that library. She said, "Correct."

I can't even play a radio. I try to get a certain station and I can never get it. I either end up with that station in Rochester that broadcast pantomimes or Radio Moscow. With TV, it's worse. Of course, our set at the monastery is so old it shows only "I Love Lucy." The reception is so bad that the other night I watched the test pattern for twenty minutes without realizing it.

I was given a laptop computer as a gift. It was inscribed, "From the Bilsbough Writers Society to Brother Craig in gratitude for your resignation." Brings a tear, doesn't it? It took me two years to figure out the laptop. But then I got it open. I thought it would work like an Etch-A-Sketch, but it didn't. I even took an eighteen-week course that met Monday through Saturday. After that, I knew how to turn it on. I also know how to delete but not how to type anything.

I have a real problem with machines even as simple as washing machines, dryers, dishwashers and my electric napkins. I just wish they would make machines simpler or make them stupider so I can identify with them. Last week I spent three nights in a row reading the directions for assembling an electric toenail clipper.

When I buy an electric gadget, the clerk always does three things that annoy me: 1. Smiles like a newscaster doing a charity benefit. 2. Says, "Now, here's your receipt" as if I was perhaps thinking I was receiving the key to the city of San Diego. 3. Says, again while smiling, "My, you have purchased a very user-friendly product." That's the last thing I ever get. It never gets to be friendly because I never get to use it. What I want is an Idiot-Proof product. Something that only needs to be plugged in—not even taken out of the box.

Another time, it was a door-to-door salesman's fault. "Good day to you, sir. You look like the kind of person who can't pass up the deal of a lifetime." I smiled and kept eating crackers. "Today we have for you our brand new, lightly patented, E-Z electric tie presser. Yes, sir, it does neckties, bow ties, ascots and apache. It beats every other model. It comes in first place—the others don't even tie! Little humor there, sir," he said as he adjusted his monocle. "Now, sir, for the limited time of ten years, we are selling these machines at only $39.95, and if you act right now, before I stop talking, you get a free carrot crusher, a subscription to *Popular Pudding Magazine* and one piece of plastic rainproof siding for your house." So I bought one. "Thank you, sir. I'll go to my truck and bring it on the dolly." It took me eight weeks to assemble it. Then I realized that monks don't wear ties. Oh, well, that's life!

That's Life!

As a monk I don't watch much TV. But yesterday I had a cold, so I stayed in bed in front of the TV—for about twelve hours. Here's what I watched:

The Local News — A story about a man who can scream for an hour without stopping to breathe and one about a kid who makes kites out of old toasters.

Maggie Magee Talk Show — Today's guest had her house burned down (by a friend), and she is suing the match company. The audience insulted her with remarks about negligence such as—"You should have been home." Her friend was on the show and said that she had a right to burn people's houses. It was her way of expressing affection. The host agreed. I've never understood how anyone could go on those talk shows and discuss how overweight they are and have the host say, "We're insulting you, stupid, to try to help you."

Big Bucks Basket — A new game show where guests have to guess how many bucks are in the basket, then roller skate over to the Big Bucks Basket Button and be the first one to push it. One lady won $8,000 and a lifetime supply of frozen okra. The other contestants just got the okra.

Mudmyer Manor — A new soap opera about a rest home in Iceland. Today Mrs. Liefsen broke a fingernail.

Happy Harry — A kids' show with a ninety-eight-year-old ventriloquist and his llama puppet. Harry talks in English and the llama (Larry) responds in Aztec. Kids must really love it.

The Evening News — "Congress has passed a bill stipulating that from now on all the bills it passes will be bills that will be passed or else bills that will not be passed, pending the Senate's approval," says Ronda Rodney, live from the White House.

Then I watched reruns of "Car Fifty-Four, Where Are You?"

then "Sea Hunt" and "Lassie." Then a sitcom filmed before a live (thank goodness) audience; "The Fernfell Family." The half-hour show involved eighteen separate arguments and 280 insults.

The evening movie was "Murder at the Wash-o-Matic," with Bette Davis, Joan Crawford and Jackie Gleason; a very artistic film, all in black and white with Greek subtitles—a wonderful musical.

Then (finally), the eleven o'clock news: "This evening Brian Boru looks at a man in Seattle who is helping his family during a time of unemployment, by going to work." After the National Anthem, sung by a British Honor Guard, the TV exploded. Now my cold is gone. So is the TV. Oh, well, that's life!

That's Life!

The latest thing is frugality. There are books on saving money, newsletters, cheapskate clubs and a video called "A Penny Slaved" that sells for $49.95. Now, don't get me wrong (people always do), I'm all for saving money, and I'm grateful for nifty-thrifty ideas, but some of them just go too far. Here's a few.

— Need a birthday gift? Give last year's telephone book wrapped in pretty newspaper.

— Why use a whole staple when a half would do?

— Eat only once every three days at an all-you-can-eat-restaurant.

— Give up golf, movies and driving to work. Sell your bed and sleep on the floor.

— Spend each vacation working!

— Earn $2 an hour teaching skydiving at home!

— Save all empty cans, milk cartons, egg containers and all packaging material. Then start a drivethru landfill service right at home!

— Call everyone collect. If they won't pay to talk to you why should you call them?

— Take your kids out of school and have them watch "Sesame Street" instead (on a TV at Sears, of course).

Here's an easy and cheap way to make neckties for your husband:

— Save all wire twist'ems from bread wrappers.

— After you have collected about 2,907, carefully weave them into a necktie.

— Trim the edges with a blowtorch.

— Apologize to your husband.

Other super saving tips include—

— Join a wholesale club and learn to eat breakfast cereal at every meal.

— Have a party and charge all the guests.

— Make your own granola from leftovers. Simply mix together cucumber skins, carrot tops, finely chopped scrap paper, and cover with a layer of used coffee grains. Bake in the sun for one year!

— Never pay full price. Argue with every store manager and sales clerk.

— Save gasoline. Ride everywhere in a friend's car.

— Keep your heat on very low, in cold weather, about thirty degrees. Research has shown that oil is more expensive than cold medicine.

For an economical vacation, try these:

— A bus trip to the local library.

— A tour of a nearby eraser factory.

— A walking tour of your yard.

— Several days riding on the Staten Island Ferry.

— A visit to a used car lot.

— Volunteer to carry luggage on a cruise to nowhere.

— Redecorate your room like a motel, by adding an uncomfortable mattress, a desk without a desk chair and a painting of three dozen sunflowers. Add a coffee mug, and scatter nine ashtrays and three nonsmoking signs around the room.

I don't think these ideas help much. In fact, I think they are worse than having a credit card. Oh, well, that's life!

*Who needs cookies? I'd rather have
a raw onion sandwich!*

The Weight Debate

(This was written when I weighed 237 pounds (I'm 5'7") Later, I lost 114 pounds and wrote a book called *Love Yourself, so ... Hate the Weight*, published by Woodbridge Press, which is also the publisher of this book you're holding.)

Weight loss is a very popular subject, and there are many learned authorities. Miss Piggy says, "Never eat more than you can lift." And Totie Fields taught, "It's time to go on a diet when the man from Prudential offers you group insurance." And Bob Hope says, "Middle age is when your age starts to show around the middle." And that great comedienne and witty woman of wisdom, Phyllis Diller, tells us, "Exercise is not my best thing. First of all I'm not built for it. My reflexes are slower than a turtle on Sominex."

I've really been trying to lose weight. I need to trim off only about a hundred pounds. Just a little toning, really. I tried dieting. I tried every diet. I bought every diet book. One said eat whatever you want, all you want, but don't eat fruit on Thursday if Jupiter is blocking the view of Saturn. The book came with a calendar and a telescope. I gained thirty-five pounds.

One book said you could eat anything you like—just eat twenty-seven grapefruit after it. I could eat only sixteen each time. I gained eighteen pounds.

Another book proposed the "think" method. It's not what you eat, it's just what you think. Think thin and you'll be thin. I gained twelve pounds and got a headache.

One book explained that it was improper food mixing that caused my weight problem. Food must be eaten according to color: white food all together, green food together at one meal and for dessert, a dish of black beans. I gained seven pounds.

Then I got a video that was supposed to really do the trick. The very skinny host explained very slowly and very simply (presuming that fat people are also stupid) that the whole problem was our eating habits. Just stop it. At least for eight weeks, don't eat. The only thing I lost from that was the price of the video.

But I refused to visit a Psychic Counselor specializing in Creatively Weighed People (the new term for fatso). There were eighteen sessions. The first one cost $588 and the rest would be free. When he's asked why the rest are free, the psychic says, "No one ever comes back." A friend went, and said the psychic went into a trance (after he got the money). Then he channeled King Tut, Queen Elizabeth I, Lillian Gish and Knute Rockne. He said, "Choose," and then made a pun about being the "channel with many channels." My friend chose King Tut who explained in hieroglyphics that, although my friend was fat, he should accept himself for what he is. My friend told him he just wanted less to accept. Anyway, that wouldn't work.

I tried an exercise class at the local library. The teacher was a nice guy named Raphie who said we'd start easy with: 400 situps, 200 pushups, a four-mile sprint and a three-legged race around the state border. I did only one exercise—I walked out. I went home and wrote a long, teary letter to Richard

Simmons, telling him how insulted I had been walking home from that class. I heard one kid say to another, "Hey, that guy is as big as a house." If that wasn't bad enough, the other kid said seriously, "I thought it was a house. That's why I threw the newspaper at him!"

"Only if we are secure in our beliefs,
can we see the comical side of the universe."
Flannery O'Connor

What the world needs is more laughter!

Mirth Ministry

A few minutes ago I founded what is called Mirth Ministry. So far I'm the only member. Let me know if you want to join! Members of Mirth Ministry bring humor and laughter into the lives of others. This can really be a beautiful ministry, bringing joy into the lives of others—children, lonely or depressed people, the sick, etc.

Helping people with humor and laughter is becoming a popular thing. There are now clown ministries that visit hospitals and some hospitals have people who go around with Comedy Carts stocked with funny things to cheer up the patients. Many doctors and nurses are advocating the value of humor for health and recovery. And rabbis, priests, ministers and even monks are getting into the act!

There are many ways you can use humor to help people. One way I think of, right off, is for the benefit of the lonely and especially the lonely elderly. Visit lonely people, and don't just chitchat—make them laugh! Tell jokes, funny stories and do funny things.

To be a well prepared Minister of Mirth, you should have a humor collection. In a box or closet, keep all kinds of funny things that you will use in your ministry. Collect the funny stories and jokes you read or hear. Buy wholesome, funny videos and audiotapes. Be sure to collect funny props. I have funny hats. I have a jester's hat, a clown hat and a great big red-with-white, polka-dot top hat with a matching giant necktie!

Realize that when you go out to bring mirth to people, say, at a rest home, you don't even need to know the people. You can go to the home and ask if there is anyone there who needs a visit. There you will find many lonely people longing for a visit—and they will surely enjoy a visit from a Minister of Mirth!

When you bring mirth and laughter into the lives of others, you also give yourself a great feeling of doing a valuable good work. I have been very happy to hear, after one of my humor talks , that there would be refreshments. No, that's not it—I was happy to be told by a widow that she has finally laughed and is so grateful for that healing laughter. Some people at my talks laugh until they cry, and the crying part is healing, too. A man with marriage problems told me, "I haven't laughed this much in six months." And many more people have told me that my funny words have helped and consoled them. And that makes *me* happy.

I have learned from experience that humor and laughter are profound, wondrous and mysterious things. They bring healing, consolation, and the strength to start life over again, the strength to pick up the pieces and carry on—not just to continue in a dragging-along sort of way, but to lift up ones head and to lift up one's heart and to smile, laugh and face life with enthusiasm, joy and chutzpah!

I often think of what a great influence the enthusiastic attitude toward life in several musical comedies was for me as I was growing up. Auntie Mame taught me to "open a new window, open a new door" each and every day. Mrs. Dolly Levi (as in Hello) taught me to "put on my Sunday clothes when I felt down and out" and to desire to "live and give" before the parade passed me by! And Fanny Brice advised that I let "no one, no, no one rain on my parade." And, finally, the Unsinkable Molly Brown taught me to be, well, unsinkable.

What does all this have to do with humor? A lot. All those ladies had a great sense of humor. They laughed at themselves, laughed at life and it's difficulties and, most of all, they made other people laugh. They were Ministers of Mirth.

I'll never forget the time I visited an old friend from my high school days. I could see that he seemed sad. So I decided that, before that visit was over, I would make him laugh at least once. Just once, even if I had to stay three weeks and pay him to laugh. So I tried jokes. No good. He'd heard them. (One he'd told me in high school.) Then I tried funny stories. No laugh. Then comic routines—you know, one funny remark after another, like: "Boy, the economy is so bad that the other day I bought a pound cake and it was only eleven ounces!" Nothing. Not even a smile. Then I got desperate. I thought of lighting his curtains on fire, but then realized that there wasn't anything funny about that. So I said, "Now, before I go, just for old time's sake, I'm going to sing a song." He remembered my singing. He laughed. He roared. He held his sides. I left.

Yes, bring laughter into the lives of others. Yes, friends, and be sure to take Geritol, and remember, the more you laugh the more you laugh.

"Become a child again. Laugh!"
Barbara Johnson

And just what are you laughing at!

I Hate Women's Magazines

Of course, to be happy and very self-helpish, we should all help others and try to make our world a better place. I, as a humanitarian, being civic minded, and as a leader of world cultural enrichment and as a member of the U.N. Committee on Plastic Wrap (U.N. meaning here Unshelled Nuts), I have founded the Society for the Prevention of Stupidity, which has as its goals:

— The elimination of the U. S. Government
— The promotion of color-coordinated dental floss.
— The absolute outlawing of women's magazines.

I hate women's magazines. They are stupid. I can prove it. Why, just look at the covers. I have a set of encyclopedias that contain less than these covers promise. Take any of them: say, "Women's Pages" or "Family Folios," as examples. Can't you just imagine the covers!

— "Lose 100 lbs. in Two Weeks Without Dieting or Exercising."

— "You and Your Family Can Live on $2 a Week."

— "Learn Cross-stitch, Needle Point and Polo all in One Evening."

— "White House Pastry Chef Shares His 200 Favorite Chocolate Chip Cookie Recipes."

Then you open the magazine and spend an hour reading the ads. Total loss of time. I get so confused. Once, I went to the store and asked for "Oil of Olay" peanut butter.

Another thing that gets me: why should I spend my time reading about people's inconsequential deeds? Who needs articles like:

— "A woman who cares: Marge Barge, founder of the Hang Nail Helpers Society."

What also bugs me is this: the articles are about articulate, intelligent, well-educated women. But the ads encourage life commitment and financial investment to keep one's fingernails moist. Or is it skin?

Or, there's an article about a lady who runs a home for alienated amoebas (and needs donations), and the ad next to it says for *only* twenty-eight payments of $29.95 (plus shipping and handling, and not available in Wisconsin), you can get a porcelain plate with a nationally unknown artist's painting of Shirley Temple, Grover Cleveland and Lassie.

No, I really don't like those magazines. Too many photos of people with straight teeth and 1.5 children.

Another thing. Those helpful hints. Ridiculous. Things everyone knows:

— "Sandblast your bathtub once a week to remove mold, mildew and loose tiles."

— "If you iron your toes each evening, they won't curl."

— "Don't allow visitors, and you won't have to clean your house."

— "Princess explains how she removes wax buildup from her kitchen floors."

Also, the recipes! Julia Child is needed to orchestrate them! Yet they promise:

— "Ten-Minute Dinner Party for Twenty. Just Heat and Throw."

— "How To Make Leftover Beans into Fettuccini Alfredo."

— Goodbye, Fondue! Hello, Blowtorch Barbecues."

— The King of Oman's Favorite Soup."

— Carol Burnett's No-cook Ice Water."

— Six Hundred No-calorie Desserts from Cordon Bleu."

And the crafts! They really upset me. First of all, the ones in the picture look as if they were made by a team from the Smithsonian led by Martha Stewart. My finished product looks like play-dough after it's been through therapy. My "Holiday Welcome Mat" took me six weeks (from "Twenty Crafts You Can Make in One Evening"). It was mistaken by more than one visitor for my mailbox. And the directions! (Which are always continued on Page 159.) There were 3,000 words in small print. I was told to "enlarge the pattern given for the 8,000 pointed star, using a square, ruler, a tripod and a government grant."

And the family articles!

— "How I Stopped My Six-Year-Old Daughter from Running for Congress."

— "Krissy at the Boston Symphony: a Two-Year-Old's Violin Recital."

— "Teaching Toddlers the ABC's, Sharing and Icelandic Sagas."

— "No Child of Mine Will Have Staticky Socks!"

And the financial helps! I just can't believe it. Again and again, I read things like:

— "Earn Millions Selling Grape Soda Door-to-Door."

— "How One Woman Earned 1.28 Million a Week Teaching Knitting Over the Telephone."

And the ads! They are the worst. Totally unbelievable:

— "Avoid money scams. We'll tell you how. Send us $285.95, your credit card number, bank account number and a sample of your signature."

Or this one:

— "Earn tons of extra income cooking bread sticks at home."

And the free offers! Stuff nobody would want or need!

— "The U. S. Department of Agriculture will be happy to send you a free book listing the middle names of all the onion growers in Utah."

— "One paper clip, two elastic bands and several pieces of scrap paper will be sent free. Send a S.A.S.E. to 'Oliver's Office Starter.'"

— "Like Herbal Tea? Send for a tiny free sample. Please add $4.95 for postage and handling."

Or those deals where you get lots of stuff for $1:

— "Real perfume from the real Paris (France) for only $1. Send before July 32nd and receive a set of the *Encyclopedia Britannica,* a 'Father Knows Best' video and a trip for two to Tierra del Fuego."

— "1,400 CD's for $1. You must promise to invest heavily in our company, pay our debts and get us out of bankruptcy."

And all the causes and commemorations we are urged to be committed to:

— "Denver Woman Starts Home for Retired Philosophers."

— "Help Your Local Bar. Please Donate Ice."

— "Her Anger Lead Her to Action. How Clavena Cliver Started the Society to Stop Giggling."

— "This Tuesday, Join Us in Celebrating Volcano Awareness Day."

— "Remember, This is National Dental Floss Salesman Week."

What really bothers me is all those annoying tear-out cards that get in the way! Just tear out, mail, no postage necessary, and you'll soon receive eighteen issues (all at once) to "Himalayan Highway," Tibet's most popular road-construction magazine.

Yes, I hate women's magazines. But I do hope one of them will someday accept an article I send in.

Maybe this Memory Module Upgrade
will help me remember.

Computers Are Handy Paperweights

I recently went to the Springfield, Massachusetts computer show, because Brother John Raymond, a computer genius, wanted to go. (He's the author of *Catholics on the Internet*, published by Prima Publishing, $19.95 plus $2 for postage from our monastery—the address is at the end of this book. End of infomercial.) I am a complete moron when it comes to computers. I went to the show because I thought there might be food.

I spent the whole time confused. I had no idea what I was looking at, except the carrying cases. Although I did have what I thought was a brilliant idea. Instead of a laptop computer, for very fat people, they should make an ab-rest computer. I told Brother John. He tried to lose me in the crowd.

One booth was selling memory. I did not know you could buy it. I ran over to an exhibit that I thought was of "bored mothers." But it was about "motherboards." Again and again, I stared at things I had no understanding of: sound cards, modems (or modi or Mordecai) and ink jet de-cloggers. Excited, I gave a friendly wave to a familiar roll of duct tape.

In a dazed state, I wandered around and was disappointed when I tried to buy some chips for a snack. I thought they were potato chips. One booth featured enough cable for Martha Stewart to macrame a border around Greenland. A man assured me that this computer show was a good deal for people who want to build their own computer. (An ambition I have never had.) I tried to buy software with service for six. I'll tell you one thing. I never saw so many Asians outside of Chinatown. They all were buying and selling with great expertise. I wonder what they'll be like when they're old enough to start school.

I did get concerned when I found myself staring into the rubbish. There I saw many familiar things. One thing that amazed me is that one booth was selling small gargoyles. I'm sure that, to computer people, that make sense.

Brother John was off looking at a chord-less keyboard that can be attached to a treadmill; it sends work to the office by radio waves, satellite and several volunteer carrier pigeons. Then I went to a booth that had a very big sign that read "Books." But all the books were written in that computer jargon that makes James Joyce seem like a nursery rhyme. The titles were impressive: "Gigabyte RAM for French Windows 99"; "Downloading and Upgrading for IBM, Mac and the PTA"; "Surf the Net, E-mail and Design Your Own Rambo Paper Dolls"; "Windows 97, Doors 98, and Those Shutters that Have Been Around Since 1964."

I looked at some CDs: "Gourmet Meal Planner with 58 Ways To Do Radish Rosettes"; "Trace Your Family Tree, Balance Your Check Book and Organize Your Bread Bag Collection"; "Great Works of Literature: Shakespeare, Mark Twain, the Encyclopedia Icelandica and the Collected Recipes of Eva Braun"; and "Everything Written in English Since Tuesday, July 5, 1942."

I ask a woman selling books if she understood all the books, and she said, "No." I told her that Brother John calls me, not old fashioned, but Neanderthal because I still write with a pen. She commented kindly, "At least, you're not a hunch-back." What, tell me, was that supposed to mean?

At last, it was time to go. Working our way through the crowd, I was looking forward to getting outside, getting to the car and reading an old fashioned book like "Jane Austin's Poems, Hand-printed Replica of the Original Embroideries." Brother John enjoyed the show. All the way home he expounded in some technical language that I doubt has been written down, at least not with the pen. By the way, at the computer show there was no food.

Grim care, moroseness, anxiety—all this rust of life
ought to be scoured off by the oil of mirth.
Mirth is God's medicine.
                              Henry Ward Beecher

Why can't I have cosmetic surgery?

Who Is The World's Funniest Monk?

As the unproclaimed "Minister of Mirth," as someone who has dedicated his life to making people laugh (whether they like it or not), as the only monk to have written a book called *Humor Helps!,* I have decided to share with the world, etc., my goal, my dream, my destiny—wherein lie all my hopes and desires. (At least for this afternoon.)

My ambition is to be the world's funniest monk. Okay, the competition isn't tough, given all that silence.

Being a monk is great, but things can get confusing. I mean, sometimes people can't quite grasp what a monk is. I once filled out a form for the telephone company and, for occupation, I wrote "monk." (It was either that or "professional prayer.") A week later I got a call from the phone company and the woman very sternly asked, "Sir, why did you state your occupation as 'skunk?'" I told her it was monk.

Another confusion is about the habit I wear. People have seriously and not unkindly called it a robe, gown or dress. One woman pulled her car over and scolded me for going for a walk in my bathrobe. Once, I got my habit caught getting on a train. One woman suggested, "Why don't you tie up your dress." I told her that if I did that all the time it might become a habit. Sometimes it's on an envelope addressed to our monastery, where the most confusion occurs. Once, instead of reading "Cloistered Monastery," the envelope read "Clustered Monsters," though there was some truth to that.

Sometimes I wake up in the middle of the day and just can't believe I am a monk. I mean, I can't believe I was accepted. I have Brother Contracticus to thank for that. He's my superior. He kindly overlooked the fact that I had only three qualifications for becoming a monk:

— I'm Catholic.
— I've seen "The Sound of Music" eighteen times.
— I have an autographed picture of Loretta Young.

But I'm sure Brother Contracticus has, now and then, regretted letting me join. Like when he asked me to think of something we could make at the monastery, something to make money. Some monks make jelly; others make fudge. My project was a complete disaster. I invented unbreakable peanut brittle. "But it's supposed to break," said Brother Contracticus, who went on to slowly explain that brittle means: it breaks. My next attempt was to open a little restaurant at the monastery. I'm afraid it wasn't very popular. It was a self-serve, all-you-can-eat, whipped-cream restaurant. Then I tried setting up a plastic refinishing workshop. I was amazed at how few people wanted their microwave dishes refinished.

But Brother Contracticus is good to me. Yes, he's a bit stern, gruff and serious. But he has a good heart—by which I mean he's never had a bypass. I explained to him that the monastery could make some money if I went out to work. He said, "Fine," but asked what kind of work I wanted to do. I suggested:

— Professor of Philosophy
— Advisor to the President
— Librarian.

Brother Contracticus laughed. (The first time I ever saw him do that.) Then he suggested comedy—and he was serious. So I packed a small suitcase and set out. I've now performed all over the country—sometimes before an audience. So far I've earned $12.95. Not bad for a monk, really.

A lot of people thought it was very strange for a funny guy like me to become a monk. Then a lot of people thought it was strange that a monk would do comedy. Well, as Abraham Lincoln didn't quite say, "You can please none of the people none of the time." Anyway, here I am—a monk and a kneel-down comic. Of course, it means I've had to give up my other career—advocating for the rights of green mold.

Of course, there are some advantages in being a monk and a comic. If you don't laugh, I won't pray for you. Also, I have extra help. I pray to St. Eutropalis. He's the patron saint of comedians—he was a politician. Prayer is a wonderful thing. When I was a kid, I always prayed that I'd grow up to be a great person like Wally Winfreed, the man who decided that a green label means decafe.

Here I am, doing comedy, making people laugh, making people forget that they're in debt, overweight and overworking. That's it—my mission is temporary amnesia. I should get a 900 number. Yes, indeed. I want to make people laugh so much that they forget their worries, their troubles and where they parked their car.

But I do try to help people, if not with my act at least by the counseling I do after the show. I spend hours just listening—while people insult me. People love to insult me. It's gotten so I compliment other people just so I can, at least, hear compliments. After every gig I get at least one insult. And people pick the strangest things to insult. One lady said, "Brother, I think your act would be a lot funnier if you changed your eye color." Or, a guy once said, "You're not very funny. I find the old Lassie show was much funnier." That really hurt. Or, take the letter I got the other day. "You're a lousy comic. You're not funny. You should try something you're more talented at—like dry cleaning." How could Aunt

Twaddle write something like that? Anyway, insults or not, I'm a monk and a comic.

I mean, Gregor Mendel was a monk and a scientist; Thomas Merton, a monk and a writer. Why can't I be a monk and a comedian? I truly believe I'm making people happy. Why, just the other, day a lady smiled at me on the subway—you see, that's proof. I'm almost certain she wasn't the one who pick-pocketed my wallet—even though she bumped me four times.

I'm sure I'm making some people happy, at least the monks back at the monastery—because I'm away a lot. I'm always sure to send them postcards with notes like:

"I'm fine. Hope you're having a very silent time. Don't say 'Hello' to everyone for me, as that would break the silence.

"I'll be home soon, and I brought everyone a souvenir hood that has 'Epcot' written on it. I surely do miss not talking with all of you. Chant one for me.

Brother Craig"

Or, sometimes I call home. It's almost always old Brother Thomas who answers. He is hard of hearing. (That means he finds it too hard to bother to hear.)

"Good afternoon. This is Brother Thomas and not a machine speaking."

"Hello, Brother. This is Brother Craig."

"No, I'm sorry, he's away."

"No, *I'm* Brother Craig!"

"How humble of you to admit it."

"I'm just calling to let you know I'm fine."

"You've been fined? Again?"

"No, I'm fine."

"So it's not Brother Craig. Mr. Fine, what do you want?"

"Brother Thomas, it's Brother Craig, and I just called to say, 'Hello.'"

"You called to say, 'Hello.' Well, that's a waste of money."

"Well, Brother, I've got to go. I'm at a pay phone at a truck stop, and someone wants to use it."

"You got a day loan and your luck stopped and you want some Renusit?"

"No, Brother, I'm calling from a truck stop. Truck stop!"

"Why call me? I can't stop a truck from here. Tell the driver."

"Brother Thomas, someone wants to use the phone."

"Someone is using it. You are."

"Never mind, he walked away. I'll say, 'Goodbye' now."

"You didn't have to warn me. I was expecting that eventually."

So, you can see why I don't call home much. It must be all that silence. The one thing I do like about being a comic is that I get to travel—buses aren't that bad. But why does every bus have some guy who talks nonstop to the driver? And he always sits in back! One thing that's tough is the motels I have to sleep in. Oh, the rooms are okay; they're clean, the beds are fine. It's just the paintings on the wall I can't stand. The other thing I don't like is that the switch for the lamp is so far from the bulb. And those cords for the curtains that are on pulleys—I always have to yank them, then they slip and I feel like I'm playing a bass violin.

Another thing I don't like about motels is that they are getting so they charge for everything. One motel I stayed at had a sign which read:

> Ice is $1.
> TV is $2 per show.
> Sleeping in the bed is $40 extra.

Or, another place I stayed at, in order to watch TV, you have to put in a quarter. To put on a light, another quarter. To get out of the room was fifty cents!

I'd rather be at the monastery. At least, there I didn't have to pay $65 for a hard bed. But at the monastery, Brother Contracticus always ignores my "Do not disturb" sign. And he tore up my sign that read, "Please clean room now."

There are some disadvantages to being a monk who travels. Some people have some idea of a monk but only know about Gregorian chant, silence and making cheese. One lady asked if she could talk to me directly. And once, a young man in an airport said, "I just wanted to meet you. I've never met a monk before. You're in such an unusual profession." So I asked him what he did—he was a lawyer who didn't charge! Children sometimes have wonderful reactions to meeting a monk. I've been called (when I was fat) "Friar Tuck." Recently one kid said, "Hey, Mommy, look—it's Obe Wan Kenobe!" His mother was embarrassed, so she apologized, saying, "You'll have to excuse him—he's never met a religious fanatic before."

Especially in airports I'm often mistaken for a member of an Eastern religion. (I should tape Bingo cards to my luggage so people will know I'm a Catholic.) The real problem is that people come up to me and ask me questions about meditation, metaphysics and the oneness of all things. Patiently, I put down my copy of "Country Music Trivia" magazine and explain that:

— I'm not a guru.
— I've never been to India.
— I love New York City.
— My idea of transcendental is an ocean liner.
— I often buy lottery tickets.

Usually this works. But one young woman persisted. She had flowers in her hair and macrame eyeglasses. "But, surely, you can tell me if I exist or not." I assured her that she did. "But how do you know you exist?" she shot back. I asked her to trust me. She seemed relieved and asked me if I had any incense with me. "No," I responded, "but I do have some Aqua Velva." She walked away, disgusted that the highest my higher consciousness reaches is when I run too fast.

Another time (again in an airport!), a man asked if I would enlighten him regarding being, non-being, being a non-being and not being a being. He was "be-ing" so much I started to wish for honey. I asked him to be more specific, as I offered him some Cracker Jacks (he refused). He said that he wanted simply to fully comprehend the one and the many, the many and the one and the one without too many. I looked at my watch. No good, still an hour before my flight. I said, trying to sound deep, "Have you asked Miss Manners?" (He'd never heard of her.) So I took the plunge and tried to be as metaphysical as I could: "You see, my son, the way to enlightenment is simple. You must first let your mind think, therefore you am." Then I told him to read a little Kierkegaard, Julia Child and lots of Andy Rooney; for, after all, as an enlightened one once said, "There's no place like home." With tears in his eyes he thanked me and gave me a dollar.

There are other times when people think I'm not a real monk. Brother John and I went to an office equipment show, and someone really thought we were actors promoting IBM—like on their Brother Dominic commercial. Another time, someone asked if I were in the new movie being filmed nearby. I said, "No," but they wouldn't believe me. They were filming Rocky XVIII. Once, someone was convinced I was the Sultan of Sultania; another time, Billy Crystal; and, another time I was mobbed by a crowd who thought I was Michael Jordan!?

But being a monk is great. I mean, who else can make a living just praying? In a way, being a monk is a lot like being a comic. Both take a lot of faith and prayer. I actually *believe* I'm funny, and I *pray* that the audience will laugh. To answer the original question (see chapter title): Who's the world's funniest monk? It's Brother Contracticus.

"Stop laughing and listen."
George Burns

I give haircuts and I give sharp advice.

Dear Abbey ...

People do have problems. And then, usually, people consider their problems a problem. That's the real problem with problems. Now, St. Catherine of Siena said—and I'm translating freely—"So, what's a problem? All problems end with death." Of course, I have great empathy with people's problems. I used to have great sympathy, but then sympathy went out of style. So now I have empathy, only I don't know what it is. Now, I guess I'm considered a great problem solver.

Just the other day, Brother John said to me—"You're such a problem." People write to me here at the monastery and ask me for advice. I feel like Abby at the Abbey. Anyway, I thought I'd share with you some of my responses. You may be so impressed with my wisdom, sage advice and general smartness that you'll want to write to me. Please include a SASE (Sizable Annuities, Stocks, Estates) and allow nine years for a response.

Dear Brother,

My girlfriend likes to go to restaurants that serve nouvelle cuisine. The last time, I was served one carrot (in a balsamic vinegar glaze), three and a half peas and a sprig of parsley. As I work at the docks all day, I get hungry. My girlfriend doesn't like the fact that I bring along a cooler filled with real food like bread, bananas and marshmallow fluff to supplement the $19.95 scrap of a meal those rip-off restaurants serve. Am I wrong?

Hungry in Hoboken

Dear Hungry,

Although many states have outlawed nouvelle cuisine—because the spindly carrot spikes that usually stick out of the chocolate mousse are considered dangerous—I guess that where you live it is still allowed. Nouvelle cuisine is responsible for chefs putting a microscopic morsel of cake made of hazel nuts on top of some watered-down raspberry jam and then they always swirl—using a plastic mustard dispenser—a tablespoon of liquefied portobello mushrooms. And the price! You leave the restaurant hungrier then when you went in. All those bucks just for snooty atmosphere, new age music and waiters with ponytails. I mean, when you're hungry you want food—real food—not undercooked stuff cut in hexagonal shapes all for the sake of the "presentation." So anyway, no, you are not wrong.

Brother Craig

Dear Brother Craig,

My name is Louise. Please settle an argument. My friend, Louise, says (she lives here in Boca Raton, too)... she says my fake Roman coin jewelry doesn't go with my pink jogging suit. We walk at the mall each morning. Now my other friend (her name is Louise, also)—the three of us walk each morning, except on Tuesday when I volunteer at the cholesterol clinic—anyway, she says that Louise says my jewelry looks gorgeous. But that's no help since that Louise says everything is gorgeous. I mean, she buys all her stuff from the shopping channel: her jewelry, her clothes and even her mobile home. Anyway, she says they are gorgeous, but I don't know. So I thought I'd write to you. I saw you on TV once. Such a cute monk, a nice boy. Anyway, what do you think?

Louise

Dear Louise,

Well, I must say, I think Louise is correct.

Brother Craig

Dear Brother,

I attended one of your talks. I've since recovered. I was confused by something you said. How can you claim that tapioca is the meaning of life?

Confused

Dear Confused,

When I said that Tapioca was the meaning of life, I think I meant that the large pearl tapioca was the meaning of life. That, I think, we should establish right off. We are talking about the large pearl variety. Now, I think it all becomes clear when we recall that tapioca is sweet and tastes good and is fat free. So that makes it—as Heidegger would say, quoting Wittgenstein to Kierkegaard, the "Thing in Itself." And, by that I'm referring to the essence of the essential thingness or, in this case, the essential tapiocaness. Therefore, without delving too deeply into the rice pudding (messy business), or bringing in the whole Hume-Locke-Berkeley argument of apple crisp, I think we can quantitatively and ontologically state, given the groundbreaking work of Hobbs, Descartes, Spinosa and Mel Torme, that tapioca is the meaning of life. Of course, it's just a theory.

Brother Craig

Dear Brother,

I have often read the mathematical problems that people write in to that super smart lady named Marilyn. Now you do not seem to be very smart (I've seen your picture), but I thought I'd send you this math problem just to see what kind of a flako answer you would give, being as you're not too bright, as I've already said, sort of. Here is the problem. If a boat is traveling at fifteen knots per hour for three hours then doubles that speed for one hour and fifteen minutes, and then does half of the original speed times twice the doubled speed for twenty minutes, what was the dessert they served at the captain's table?

Bet I stumped you

Dear Bet,

The dessert was tapioca.

Brother Craig

Dear Brother,

My brother says that if you stand on the top of a mountain during a full moon your rice won't boil over. Is that true or is that just somebody's old wives' tale?

The sister of my brother

Dear Sis,

Your brother is absolutely correct. If you stand on the top of a mountain during a full moon your rice will not boil over, providing you are not cooking any rice at the time.

Brother Craig

Dear Brother,

My sister insists that there is no such state as Delaware, because she says you never hear anything about it on the news, you never meet anyone from there and no one really knows where it is. She seems to have a point, but I just know I've heard of it. Maybe it is a city?

Perplexed

Dear Perplexed,

Delaware is a state. Without it the Chesapeake Bay would be in Bermuda.

Brother Craig

Dear Brother,

I read in an article that you are a very shy, demure and quiet kind of person, afraid to speak in public and very bashful. Is that true?

Gladys

Dear Gladys,

It is all very true except for the fact that I'd love to be on a TV commercial and star in my own show and well, yes, I am very bashful.

Brother Craig

Brother,

Settle an argument. My sister says that Greenland never sends a team for the congo line competition at the Olympics. I say they do. What do you say?

Maggie Miller

Dear Maggie,

You're both wrong. Greenland does send a team but it's for the rumba competition.

Brother Craig

Dear Monk,

Settle an argument. My sister says you are the stupidest, dumbest, most ignorant person on the face of the earth, or at least in New England. She says you have only become famous because people have always been fascinated by monks who are funny and acrobats who grow chives—if you know what I mean. Any comment?

Richard Ridley

Dear Richard,

My comment is that, if each of us would do his or her part, we could conquer the problem of toast burning on one side and remaining uncooked on the other.

Brother Craig

Dear Brother,

My husband says I write too many letters to people asking advice. I don't agree. What do you think? Please advise.

Helen Gibson

Dear Helen,

Well, while you are not wrong, your husband certainly could be right, although your being right doesn't make his opinion wrong. (I learned this kind of answer from watching politicians on TV.)

Brother Craig

Dear Br. Craig,

I know you'd rather avoid the deeper issues of philosophy, but my question is—do you think?

Benny Smith

Dear Benny,

Sometimes I do. I really do. Like, just now I was thinking I should end this chapter. And I did.

Brother Craig

"Let your heart be merry."
Judges 19:6

What else can I say?

Epilogue

What is an epilogue? Well, it seems to me that an epilogue is where a writer puts a bunch of stuff he or she or they could have put throughout the book, but he or she or they saved it for the epilogue because he or she or they

— Wanted to make the book look longer.
— Wanted to give the book an intellectual look.
— Forgot the main point of the book until the end.
— Promised a friend to write something but forgot.
— Wanted to be sure that the American Epilogue Society is happy about the book.

So here goes. (Don't worry; it'll be short. But if I were you I'd skip reading it entirely.) In summary, what I've been trying to explain (but haven't) is:

— Have a sense of humor.
— If you've got one, develop it.
— If you ain't got one, go to Wal-Mart and buy one.
— Be funny! Make people laugh.
— Make things laugh. Even make yourself laugh.

Why? It's a mystery. (And I'm saving the answer for my next book.) But I'll tell you one reason—it will help you to be happier, more loving, more *kinderish*. Sure, maybe you've never thought about that. But perhaps you should start today. After all, you are doing all kinds of things you've never done before—you've just read a book on humor written by a monk. And it was good of you to read it (did you start on this page?). It was good of you to read it considering that I seldom stayed on the subject (see the title if you, too, forgot it). But, friends, I really do believe that humor can help one (or two of us) to be happy, and that spreading humor (try a spatula) and being funny can be an effective way to help other people, while making a fast buck. That's why I wrote this book. Thanks for reading it. You made it to the end. Do not collect $200.

Brother Craig's video "Humor and Holiness," is available from The Monks of Adoration (address is at the end of "About the Author" (turn the page). The video is $9.95—mention this book and it's only $9.94! Add $1.50 for postage. Also available is an audiotape of Brother's talk, "The Power of Positive Faith." It's $4 plus $1 for postage.

Of course, his diet book, *Love Yourself, so ... Hate the Weight!* is available from Woodbridge Press. Just call (800) 237-6053. End of commercial.

"The person who can bring the spirit of laughter into a room is indeed blessed."
Bennett Cerf

Live beaver collectors of the world, unite!

About the Author
(of this book you are holding,
or stepping on)

Brother Craig, founder of The Monks of Adoration, of Petersham, Massachusetts, is an internationally famous Catholic monk who doesn't know how to play Bingo. He has three B.A. degrees (he completed thirty-five credit hours during one semester at the University of Albuquerque, which is probably the world's record, even though three of the credits were in volleybally—the school is now closed). He has two graduate degrees in theology from the Pontifical University of St. Thomas Aquinas in Rome but can find only one of them.

Brother speaks no languages fluently. He has written, at least, five books and one play. His articles, poetry and fiction have been published in numerous magazines. Brother Craig writes several columns for various publications, including one called *Health and Nutrition*, and a humor column called "Oh, Brother!"

He is a health and fitness expert, which means he lost 114 pounds in fourteen months and wrote a book called *Love Yourself so,... Hate the Weight!*, published by Woodbridge Press. This book got Brother on many national TV shows such as "Inside Edition," "Fox on Trends," "Day and Date," "Real Life," CNN, and he was almost on "The Late Show with David Letterman." (Dave, call me.) He's been featured in numerous newspapers (Page One stories in the *Boston Herald, Boston Globe* and *USA Today*) and magazines internationally (even the *London Times*). Thus, he is frequently approached by strangers who tell him he's the monk who wrote the diet book—which he knows.

Brother Craig, the founder of Mirth Ministry, frequently speaks at conferences, giving funny talks on the value of humor. He is an enthusiastic and funny speaker, and is sometimes called the "Mirthful Monk." Many people throughout the United States and Canada have benefited from Brother's dynamic, high-energy presentation of the benefits of humor. More people, luckier still, have never attended one of his talks.

Brother Craig is a member of the Merry Christians, as well as the American Association for Therapeutic Laughter, the International Society for Humor Studies, Comedy Writers Association, and the Save the Marzipan Society. He writes humorous gags for cartoonists and for greeting cards.

When Brother Craig was in high school he actually won several awards for doing standup comedy, and each time he was so shocked he had to sit down. He also very successfully played numerous comic roles in plays and musicals, winning the Best Actor Award for his role in the senior class comedy play, the name of which Brother can't recall. He was known to bring the house down with his comic singing. But the next day he always helped put it back up.

Brother Craig's favorite color is bright yellow, he's addicted to reading self-help books and is unbearably enthusiastic. He enjoys gardening, having philosophical conversations about tapioca and collecting live beavers. In honor of becoming forty, Brother is learning how to play the piano. He is now completing (and should be finished this afternoon) a funny novel about the Middle Ages, called "Mel." He lives in America with millions of other people.

Brother Craig can be reached by casting directors for Gulden's Mustard commercials and other important people at The Monks of Adoration, P. O. Box 546, Petersham, MA. 01366-0546. E-Mail is Monkadorer@prodigy.net.

Visit his Mirth Ministry home page at http://www.monksofadoration.org/mirth.html

Brother John is such an angel!

About the Photographer

Brother John Raymond's photographs have appeared in Brother Craig's *Love Yourself, so...Hate the Weight!*, a book published by Woodbridge Press. He is talented not only with the camera but also in thinking up ideas for funny photos. Brother John is also a pro with a video camera. (He's also great at running the Boston Marathon!)

Brother John is co-founder of The Monks of Adoration, has a B.S. in mathematics, a high school teaching certificate, and an M.A. in theology from Holy Apostles Seminary.

He writes a column called "Prayer," for the *Catholic Twin Circle* and is the author of *Catholics on the Internet*, published by Prima Publishing, causing him to be called the Cyber Monk.

About Gene Perret,
Author of the Foreword

Three-time Emmy winner Gene Perret is one of America's best-known comedy writers. He has written for Carol Burnett, Bill Cosby, Phyllis Diller and Tim Conway, and is Bob Hope's No. 1 joke writer. He is the author of numerous books and is the editor of *Gene Perret's Round Table,* a newsletter. He lives in Westlake Village, California.